RISE
UP IN
ANGER

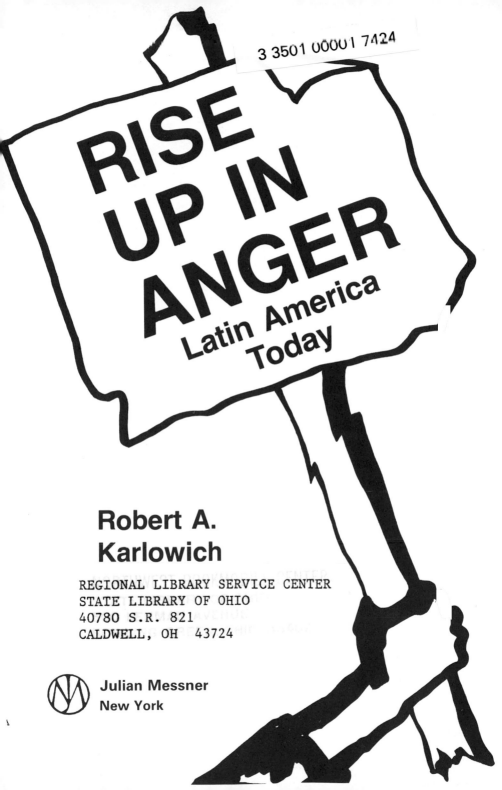

RISE UP IN ANGER

Latin America Today

Robert A. Karlowich

Julian Messner
New York

Published by Julian Messner,
A Division of Simon & Schuster, Inc.
Simon & Schuster Building
Rockefeller Center
1230 Avenue of the Americas
New York, New York 10020

JULIAN MESSNER and colophon are
trademarks of Simon & Schuster, Inc.

Manufactured in the United States of America
10 9 8 7 6 5 4 3 2 1

Design by Beverly G. Haw Leung, A Good Thing, Inc.
Maps by Mary Leto
Library of Congress Cataloging in Publication Data

Karlowich, Robert A.
    Rise up in anger.

        Bibliography: p.
        Includes index.
        Summary: Examines current social, political, and
economic problems in Latin America and puts them in
perspective by recounting their historical background.
        1. Latin America—History—1948-   —Juvenile
literature. [1. Latin America—History—1948   ]
I. Title.
F1414.2.K37   1985   980'.03   84-22646
ISBN: 0-671-46525-2

To Alex, Blake, Colin and Emily,
for a better tomorrow.

Acknowledgments

I wish to thank the following persons for their help while I was writing this book:

Tufan Bener of the United Nations, for particular economic data; Fran Bradley, assistant headmaster of The George School in Newtown, Pennsylvania, who kindly allowed me to attend a series of special lectures on Central America; personnel of the Inter-American Development Bank, especially David Mangurian, who advised about the location of photographs; Peter Kostmayer, United States Representative for the Eighth Congressional District of Pennsylvania, for providing particular data and publications about Latin America; Janet Melvin of Philadelphia, for her frank opinions and vivid descriptions of recent events she witnessed in Honduras and Nicaragua; Dr. Janet Reid and Dr. Willis Reid of the Walter Reed Army Institute of Research, for providing information about Brazil; Edward Spicer of the Palm Beach Academy in Florida, for his sound advice and guidance; Helen Szterenfeld of the International Planned Parenthood Federation, for supplying current population statistics on Latin America; and Stephen Zywalka, an evangelical missionary in Guatemala, for sharing his experiences with me.

Contents

The Latin American Continent

Every person the the United States from the youngest student up knows the name of Christopher Columbus, but not everyone is aware that he never set foot on the soil of North America. Between 1492 and 1502 he sailed to the Western Hemisphere four times. He cruised in and around many of the islands in the Caribbean, discovering present-day Haiti, Cuba, Jamaica, and Puerto Rico, among others, and he skirted the shores of Central America and of Venezuela in South America.

We in North America celebrate his discovery, even though he did not touch our continent, because he was one of the first to test the unknown seas and seek a new passage to the East. Of course, Leif Erikson, the Norseman, is credited with having reached the Western Hemisphere sometime around the year 1000, and others came before and after him. But outside the settlement of Greenland, nothing really came of those voyages.

Millions of Europeans were to follow Columbus to settle or seek their fortunes in the unknown wilds of the new lands. We name cities, institutions, streets, plazas, and even songs after Columbus, but there our relationship to him ends. North Americans look mainly to England or France for their traditions and for the roots that have determined the form and content of our society. But in the land to our south known as Latin America, from Columbus's time on, the social and religious beliefs and institutions of Spain found their way deep into the life of the people. The only other country that wielded as big an influence in the same area was Portugal, another Latin country, which lies next door to Spain.

North and South

The "Latin" separates North and South America as firmly as any physical border. It relates not only to a language difference, Spanish and Portuguese (with a sprinkling of French) as opposed to predominantly English (and some French in Canada), but also to substantially different types of colonization in the beginning. North America, especially the Northeast, was essentially settled with farm colonies by people who came to live on the land. They established in their settlements a system of government in which the landholders participated and under which people were allowed to practice their own religion. In fact, freedom of worship had been the main reason some of the early settlers came to New England, as we all know from our study of the Pilgrims. The British Crown did have authority here, though, and conflicts arose between the settlers and the British governors. The early democratic spirit endured, however, and gradually led to the American Revolution in 1776.

And what of Latin America? It was settled mainly by people from Spain who wanted to exploit the riches of the new world, men who were primarily interested in profit and adventure. To understand why this happened, we need to know a few facts about Spain.

Up to the fifteenth century, Spain was divided into two kingdoms, Aragon and Castile. They were ruled by Ferdinand of Aragon and Isabella of Castile. In 1469, the two monarchs were married, uniting the two kingdoms and bringing all of Spain under the same rule. For some seven hundred years before this occurred, the Christian people of Spain had been fighting the Islamic Moors, who had invaded and conquered the area early in the eighth century. Not until 1492, the same year Columbus set sail, were the Spanish able to drive the last of the Moors out of Granada, in southern Spain. After that, the monarchs of Spain ruled their land unchallenged. Portugal had forced the Moors off its land by 1249.

The Spanish Character

The centuries-long fight against the Moors had an effect on the character of the Spanish people. Those who fought became imbued with a strong religious and military spirit. They were defending

Christianity and the Catholic church as well as the Spanish Crown. They regarded fighting for their religion as a holy occupation. Excitement and adventure soon became a way of life for the Spanish people who had fought so long. Thus, by the time of Columbus, the Spanish warriors were tough, brave, and always ready for an opportunity to fight and to show their religious zeal, often to the point of ruthlessness and cruelty.

These were the conquistadores, the conquerors, who came to the new world from Spain to seek their fortune in Latin America. They came hoping to find wealth and glory, to spread the Catholic faith, and to escape their boredom with the peaceful life at home. They were not seeking a place where they could settle in peace; the conquistadores were not pilgrims.

Settling the Land

And what was this new world like? It was a land of striking beauty and contrasts: thick, impenetrable jungle; some of the highest mountains in the Western Hemisphere; broad, open plains; deserts; and a range of climate that included terrible, debilitating humidity in some places, and in others a mild, temperate climate that made living a pleasure. The conquistadores encountered the remnants of once great Indian civilizations—such as the Mayas in Mexico, Honduras, and Guatemala—and the still powerful Incas in South America; and the Aztecs also in Mexico. The Spanish soon subdued them all. Most important, the conquistadores found gold and silver—enough to make Spain the wealthiest country in the world for a time and a powerful maritime empire.

Fifty years after Columbus first reached what he thought was the Indies, Spain's conquistadores had subjugated the Indians and laid claim to an area that ran from Mexico down almost half the length of South America, except for Brazil, which came under the control of Portugal. Spanish explorers even pushed into the southwestern part of the present-day United States and established some settlements there. The British, French, and Dutch tried to make inroads in the new world, too, but they had to be satisfied with only a few toeholds.

One historian has pointed out that the British Crown seemed almost not to care about the colonies its citizens established around the world. Most British settlements were begun by private companies. Government officials were present, but they stepped in only when disputes arose that could not be settled between the parties.

Many early Spanish settlements were also started with money provided by rich individuals or companies who wanted to invest in the new world, but the royal authority of the Spanish Crown was vigorously exercised. Ferdinand and Isabella were in the process of consolidating their power at home, and they had no intention of allowing rival centers of authority to develop in the new world. Thus, the monarchs had strict and detailed laws about governing and taxing the settlers in the new possessions. The sixteenth and seventeenth centuries were a time of profitable trade and industry tightly controlled by the central governments of Europe, a system known as mercantilism.

Spain's colonies were usually closed to foreign trade and sometimes even to trade with one another. The colonies supplied raw materials, including gold and silver, to Spain and imported from home any manufactured goods they needed. Large plantations were created where export crops were raised: cacao, indigo, and sugar in the early period; coffee, bananas, sugar, and cotton later on. To ensure their control of the colonies, the Spanish rulers approved all administrative and ruling positions in the new world.

The Portuguese were not as fortunate as the Spanish. They found no native civilizations that had already organized the land and no precious metals to mine. They settled the territory of Brazil more slowly and gradually developed an agricultural export base there, especially in sugarcane. There was less conflict between the home country and Brazil, because the Portuguese Crown was more secure and saw no need to insist on the tight control exercised by the Spanish monarchy.

Creating a Society

The Spanish were astounded by the gold and silver they found in the new world. In order to gather this wealth, they captured thousands of Indians and set them to work as slaves in the mines. Control of the plantations was given to Spanish colonists under a system called *encomienda*, a feudal arrangement that was supposed to protect the Indians but really enslaved them to the land. While the Crown was genuinely concerned about the treatment of the natives, the settlers cared little and made few improvements in the Indians' condition.

Many of the Spanish who came to colonize Latin America in the early period stayed on. They settled down, became administrators, plantation owners, or merchants. Their Spanish heritage was important to them, and they kept their ties with the mother country. Beginning in the late sixteenth century, the Crown gave most administrative posts to members of the Spanish ruling class. These aristocrats came to America, more or less faithfully carried out their duties, and enriched themselves along with their monarchs. Some returned home to live in glory and opulence. Those who stayed on maintained their Spanish "purity" by marrying only Spanish women whom they brought from home. They encouraged their sons and daughters also to marry persons of pure Spanish blood.

From these people there grew up in Latin America an aristocracy of Spanish Americans who were not *peninsulares*—natives of Spain—but who were of pure Spanish descent and could trace their families back to the mainland. These were the *criollos*, pure Spanish natives of Latin America. In the early nineteenth century. Simón Bolívar, a member of the *criollo* aristocracy, would step out of his role as a playboy and military poseur and lead the struggle for independence from Spain among the people of present-day Venezuela, Colombia, Peru, and Bolivia.

The belief in the superiority of Spanish blood created many other distinctions. In addition to *pen-*

insulares and *criollos*, there were *mestizos*, people of mixed Spanish and Indian parentage. Some of them became the small traders and shopkeepers of the colonies. They were always dissatisfied with their treatment under the Crown, and many of them were in the forefront of the independence movements against Spain in the early nineteenth century. After independence they generally remained among the liberals, seeking more political and economic freedom than the conservatives, who came to represent the *criollo* aristocracy and landholding class.

Thousands of Indians retreated to the mountains to escape their Spanish conquerers; many, many others died as a result of ill treatment or diseases brought by the colonists. As the number of Indians dwindled, the rulers began importing slaves from Africa. The slaves, too, found their own life in the new world, eventually creating their own cultures and assimilating with some of the local peoples. Then mulattos, persons of black-white parentage, and *zambos*, people of Indian and black descent, also appeared. And those Indians who accepted the Spanish language and customs and came to live among the *criollos* were called *ladinos*.

In some countries, such as Costa Rica and Argentina, the Indians have all but disappeared. In others, such as Guatemala and Honduras, they still constitute a large part of the population and speak old Mayan dialects. In Colombia and Brazil there are primitive tribes that still live in the jungle.

In Brazil, the Portuguese imported masses of slaves from Africa. By the first decade of the nineteenth century over 2.5 million had been brought in, and by 1825, slaves made up almost half the population of the country. Slavery was finally outlawed in 1888. Today, there is a strong Afro-Brazilian culture, especially in the state of Bahia. It has been lovingly described in detail by the Brazilian novelist Jorge Amado.

The Presence of the Church

Alongside the Spanish conquistadores and the Portuguese colonists there were always Catholic missionaries who came seeking Indian souls for God. These priests helped to soften the strong hand of secular authority where treatment of the natives was concerned, though they did abide by the laws of the Spanish Crown and the teaching of the pope. Later, missionary orders grew wealthy from donations and taxes, and when revolutions occurred against the Spanish rulers in the early nineteenth century, the church, which then was the largest landholder in Latin America, at first backed the royal cause. Even after the church finally began to support the independence movements of individual countries, it remained essentially conservative. This stance created suspicion among some of the middle- and lower-class citizens, a certain cynicism about the church. But the religious nature of the Latin American people nonetheless remained strong, and Catholicism was the dominant religion. Today, Central and South America remain overwhelmingly Catholic.

Both the Indians and the blacks acceped Catholicism, but they often combined it with their own earlier beliefs. Local gods and superstitions, animism, fetish worship, and voodoo ceremonies all contrived to exist alongside the beliefs and rituals of the Catholic church. Today missionaries from many Christian religions are at work in Latin America, but so are these native traditions. Each learns to live with, or at least tolerate, the other. Sometimes even today tensions arise, however.

Tradition and Change

After the wars for independence from Spain ended in the 1820s, Latin America was free but exhausted from the effort. The region split into separate countries, and as they rebuilt their economies and societies, they retained features of the Spanish rule, which helped to determine the future. Latin America, including Brazil, had always exported raw materials to Europe. The new sovereign nations continued that practice, at the same time importing finished goods and industrial equipment in return. By not building their own industrial base, these countries became tied to the fluctuating economies of Europe and, later, the United States. In many countries land continued to be concentrated in the hands of a few families. Whether the ties were real or not, the landowners emphasized their Spanish ancestry and the traditions of Latin America. Their attitudes toward *mestizos*, blacks, and Indians, who still today are usually poor, became at best condescending and, at worst, vicious. They also resisted any change in the economic structure of the country and supported any force that promised to keep the status quo. Such attitudes made social and economic progress difficult and at times helped to reinforce the authoritarian aspects of these societies.

The armies that fought for independence were drawn from the lower classes. For the *mestizos*, soldiering then became a way to move upward; a military career offered prestige and the possibility for wealth through political control of a country or cooperation with the aristocracy. In the early nineteenth century, there also arose a type of leader called a *caudillo*, and most of the time this strongman ruled with an iron hand. Sometimes he was a military man; at other times a civilian who worked hand in glove with the military. Whatever the case, the *caudillo* represented authoritarian rule, backed by the gun.

By 1850, all the countries of Latin America—except Brazil, which retained its own monarchy until 1889—had created constitutional governments with electoral procedures. These governments were, however, primarily facades behind which various forces vied for power. The armies, the rich landowners and merchants, and the church were among the early groups that sought control by manipulating governments. A *caudillo*, for instance, might act under the guise of a democratic system, but as long as he had the confidence of the army or the backing of the wealthy families in his country, he could do as he pleased.

In order to build transportation and communications networks in their countries and to import finished goods, those in power borrowed from European governments and banks. These loans carried certain stipulations, however, such as foreign rights to control and share the profits of particular business activities. The presence of foreign capital and business also brought political intervention by foreign governments. In the nineteenth century, Britain was the strongest trading partner with Latin America. In the twentieth century, the United States has dominated the region.

As long as Latin American governments encouraged foreign intervention and there were occasional spurts of economic growth in many countries, the region was never able to shed its export-import dependency on European and American markets. By mid-twentieth century, Latin American countries had passed through several cycles of depression and recovery as a result of this tie. When the demand for their export crops declined, income also went down. But foreign debts only increased, because the countries had to continue borrowing from foreign banks to pay for needed imports. Gradually, schools of thought arose favoring a "Latin American way" to solve Latin American problems. The rich, the armies, the church, the growing labor and farmers' unions, and the political parties all offered their own solutions. There were proposals for land reform, more industrialization, less importation of goods, greater government control of the economy and society, more equitable distribution of wealth and resources throughout society, and less financial control and political manipulation by foreign governments and banks.

Many proposals cut across old class lines and became entangled in traditional racial prejudices and economic privileges. The resulting confrontations have often been violent, and too often those in political control have resorted to authoritarian solutions, for example by calling in the military. Sometimes the army voluntarily intervened to "preserve the traditions" of a country. Such actions have slowed social and economic progress in Latin America and led some opposition groups to take extreme positions, including armed revolt.

Because the United States has played an important part in the area in the twentieth century, many Latin Americans have criticized American government, industries, and banks, justly and unjustly, for their actions. Some Latin American groups have turned for answers to communism or Marxism, a formidable social force that operates best in the fertile ground of poverty and injustice. In back of this movement toward communism hovers the shadow of the Soviet Union, and this makes Latin America a scene of great international concern, because United States interests and Soviet ambitions are in conflict there. Thus, local frustrations and the maneuverings of foreign powers blend together at times, usually blurring issues and further endangering peaceable solutions.

At present, then, Latin America remains largely economically depressed; suffers from widespread social and economic inequality, extreme poverty, and authoritarian traditions; and continues under foreign economic control and political influence. In spite of this, in the last year or so some of the countries have made significant strides toward creating more democratic systems, and have hopes of more economic independence. Many observers ask how long these new governments will last. Are they just momentary pauses between rulers, as has happened in the past? Only time will tell whether the social, political, and economic forces in these countries will be able to reconcile their differences peaceably.

This book is about the interaction and influence of these various social, political, and economic forces today and the historical precedents that help account for their existence. The book is also concerned with the influence of the United States on Latin America and with the reasons why our country now evokes such mixed reactions among the populations there. Another concern of this book is the role played by the Soviet Union in the development of the region.

North Americans have long taken Latin America for granted and know little about it. Central America has been in the news lately, and some politicians fear that the United States will soon be "dragged" into a war there. However, newspapers report that many United States citizens don't even know exactly where Central America is or what its problems are.

The 1980 census revealed that the United States has one of the largest Spanish-speaking populations in the Americas, some 15 million; if illegal immigrants are added, it may be closer to 20 million. Such numbers affect our education system and our economy. Furthermore, Hispanic leaders are entering United States political life as representatives of constituencies with strong ties to Latin America. It is obvious that all Americans should know more about a region whose people represent such a large presence in their midst.

Limitations

Because it is a subject of great breadth, it is impossible to cover all aspects of Latin America. For instance, the Caribbean islands play an important part in the history of the region, but they have their separate problems, too, and different linguistic and cultural identities. Therefore, they are not treated here. Because Mexico and Costa Rica have relatively stable governments, they are not described in any detail.

Another area that will not be discussed is the cultural and intellectual achievements of Latin America. Only a few examples can suffice here to show that a rich, creative vein runs within its populations.

Latin America has produced four winners of the Nobel Prize in literature: Gabriela Mistral in 1945, and Pablo Neruda in 1971, both of Chile; Miguel Ángel Asturias of Guatemala in 1967; and Gabriel García Márquez of Colombia in 1982. In general, Latin American literature is considered among the most interesting and colorful being written anywhere and has produced such other noted writers as Jorge Luis Borges of Argentina, Carlos Fuentes of Mexico, Mario Vargas Llosa of Peru, and Jorge Amado of Brazil. It is also important to remember that there have been two Nobel Peace Prizes granted to Argentines: Carlos de Saavedra Lamas in 1936 and Adolfo Pérez Esquivel in 1980. Pérez Esquivel is still a leader in the human rights movement there.

Claudio Arrau is considered one of the world's foremost pianists and recently returned to his native Chile for a series of concerts. Heitor Villa-Lobos was a respected Brazilian composer who died in 1959. His works are based on the folk music of his country and are performed by major orchestras in the world.

Among painters, José Clemente Orozco, Diego Rivera, and David Alfara Siqueiros, all of Mexico, were leading muralists in this century and are held in high esteem for their work. Brazil has produced some outstanding modern architecture, especially in its new capital, Brasilia, and has been cited for advances in town planning. Oscar Niemeyer is one of the architects connected with this work.

Finally, we should not forget the wonderful and gay dance and music rhythms that have come to us from Latin America. They have considerably enriched our popular culture.

All these achievements, and many more, are part of the Latin American heritage, of value not only to the region but to the whole world.

The Third World of Latin America

Latin America includes all of South and Central America, covering some 7,900,000 square miles, which makes it a little more than twice as large as the United States. If we add Canada, however, then both North America and Latin America are about equal in size. One great difference between the two regions is the potential for development. Latin America has not yet really tapped the riches in its land, whereas North America is fully developed. Another important difference is the unity of the North American nations, as opposed to the diversity of the southern continent.

There are twenty-one countries in Latin America, stretching from the hot, dry region near the Rio Grande in the north, part of which serves as a border between the United States and Mexico, all the way to Tierra del Fuego, the cold and lonely southern tip of the continent, a distance of about 7,000 miles.

CENTRAL AMERICA

The whole expanse is divided into two geographical regions. The upper part is called Central America, occupying as it does a more or less central position between North and South America. It includes the territory from the lowland Isthmus of Tehuantepec in southern Mexico to the border between Panama and Colombia. While this division has geographic justification, historically it has one shortcoming. It leaves out most of Mexico and assigns it to North America. Mexico, however, is as much a part of Latin America as New England is part of the United States.

Belize, formerly called British Honduras, became independent in 1981 and is the only English-speaking nation in the area.

The climate of Central America follows the topography. The Caribbean coast, the eastern shore of the region, is a low-altitude area where heavy rains and high humidity prevail year-round. There are port cities on this coast and on the west coast as well, but these areas are not as comfortable to live in as the mountains, where most capitals are located.

South America

Below Panama lies the second part of Latin America, South America proper, a continent of vast wealth and breathtaking beauty. It comprises twelve nations of unequal size. Like Belize in the north, three states lie outside the sphere of Spanish and Portuguese traditions. One of them is Suriname, which was declared independent from the Netherlands in 1975; Dutch remains its official language. Guyana became independent from Britain in 1966, and English is the official language. The third non-Latin territory is French Guiana, an overseas department of France. All three countries exist for the most part outside the complex world of South America.

Like Central America, South America has both highland and lowland climates, only here the extremes are much greater. The Andes Mountains are the highest areas, starting in the northeast in Venezuela and Colombia, and running down the western or Pacific flank to the southern tip of the continent. They range from 19,500 to almost 23,000 feet above sea level.

The north central part of South America is on the equator, which means the area is hot and humid, a

SOUTH AMERICA

Caribbean Sea

Caracas

VENEZUELA

GUYANA
Georgetown

SURINAM
Paramaribo

FR. GUIANA
Cayenne

Atlantic
Ocean

Bogotá

COLOMBIA

Quito

ECUADOR

PERU

Lima

BRAZIL

Brasília

BOLIVIA
La Paz

Pacific Ocean

PARAGUAY
Asunción

ARGENTINA

URUGUAY

Santiago

Buenos Aires

Montevideo

CHILE

Atlantic Ocean

FALKLAND
ISLANDS

N

climate that gives rise to tropical rain forests. In the same area, the mountain regions create distinct temperature zones: the higher one goes in the mountains the cooler it gets and the less variation there is in temperature. The plateaus and valleys in the mountains are well populated, and the Indians who live there have adapted to the high, rarefied altitudes.

Besides the magnificent Andes, the best-known physical feature in South America is probably the Amazon River system, which is truly "Amazonian" in its range. It has the largest drainage basin in the world, and the Amazon River itself flows almost 4,000 miles from its source high in the Peruvian Andes to its estuaries on the Atlantic coast of northeastern Brazil, farther than the distance across the United States. The Amazon has tributaries that run 1,500 to 2,000 miles themselves. Two other river systems are the Orinoco in Colombia and Venezuela and the Paraná-Paraguay in the south. The Paraná-Paraguay stretches from Brazil through Paraguay into Argentina, where it empties into the Río de la Plata above Buenos Aires. All these river systems serve as important trade routes.

Production and Trade

Certain countries in South America are more industrialized than Central America. Venezuela, Colombia, Brazil, and Argentina, for example, are very advanced; in fact, Venezuela (along with Mexico in the north) is one of the world's major oil producers. Argentina and Uruguay have significant cattle ranches and meat-packing industries. It is here and in southern Brazil, by the way, that the South American gaucho, or cowboy, rides, a figure as romantic and envied as his North American counterpart. Many of these countries have important seaports as well.

Some countries have important mineral and ore deposits that have been useful in foreign trade. Chile, for instance, has some of the largest copper deposits in the world. Others have iron ore, zinc, bauxite, gold, or silver. But as in Central America, coffee, bananas, cotton, and sugar continue to be major products for export in South America.

Unlike these developed countries, however, some South American states are very poor. These nations are Peru, Ecuador, Bolivia, and Uruguay, which are still mainly agricultural, although Bolivia does have important tin deposits.

In spite of great efforts by the larger countries of South America to create an industrial base and free themselves from excessive dependence on imports, all of Latin America generally belongs to the Third World, like most of Asia and Africa, where economic growth is slow or non-existent and poverty endemic. Many people call these countries "developing nations," but that term is a euphemism, for there has actually been little development among them. The term "Third World" perhaps serves better. It distinguishes them from the other two "worlds" of developed capitalism— mainly the Western powers, most especially the United States and Japan—and communism— mainly the Soviet Union and its satellites.

World within a World

This is not to say there is no wealth in Latin America. It is there in abundance, but it is concentrated largely in one small group of the population. In Latin America, it is the poor who make up the real Third World. While the members of the elite increase their wealth, the poor become poorer. In 1970, it was estimated that about 40 percent of the population in Latin America (some 115 million) had an income below the poverty level, which at that time was $200 a year; $100 a year was regarded as destitute, and about 19 percent lived below that level. During the decade from 1960 to 1970, poverty was reduced from 51 percent to 40 percent of the population, but in numbers of people it remained the same. The United Nations Economic Commission of Latin America estimated that the richest 10 percent of the population controls 47.8 percent of total disposable income. The commission predicts that some 25 percent (about 120 million) of the people will still be living below the poverty line in 1990. And that is a misleading figure since even those just above the line will hardly be better off.

Such figures make us wonder whether economic growth alone can solve the poverty problem in Latin America. Illiteracy, malnourishment, early death from disease and lack of medical care, and excessive growth in population reinforce one another, serving to make it more difficult for the poor to change their lives. A look at the situation in some of the individual countries underlines this fact.

Central America

Statistics tell us that Guatemala is one of Central America's wealthiest countries, with an annual income of $1,110 per person. But that figure is misleading. Guatemala is also the most densely populated Latin American nation, and the wealth is unevenly distributed among its almost 8 million people. The usual estimate is that about 1 percent of the population owns some 60 percent of the arable land. Half to two-thirds of Guatemala's people are employed in agriculture; many of them are migrant workers who live in cities. These laborers include Indians, who constitute about 60 percent of the population. They speak some twenty-three dialects; some know no Spanish. These Indians are among the poorest people in Central America. To make matters worse, Guatemala can be expected to double its population by 2007, despite a life expectancy of only sixty years, and even though 70 babies die out of every 1,000 who are born.

Honduras is also a poor country, the second poorest in the Western Hemisphere, after Haiti. In 1981, the annual income per person was only $591. Life expectancy is low, just under sixty years, and the death rate among infants is one of the highest in the area, about 86 per 1,000 live births. The 4 million inhabitants of Honduras are expected to double in number by the turn of the century—much too fast a growth for the resources it has.

Almost 60 percent of the labor force in Honduras is engaged in agriculture. Having no oil reserves, it must, like other non–oil producing Third World countries, use up its export credits to pay for this

Gauchos roping steers in Argentina.
Inter-American Development Bank

Rio de Janeiro, Brazil.

Drs. Janet and Willis Reed

A medical office building in Brasilia, the capital of Brazil.

Drs. Janet and Willis Reed

The favela in São Paulo, Brazil.
David Mangurian, Inter-American Development Bank

A first grade class in Rio Preto, Brazil.
Inter-American Development Bank

Salvador, capital of the state of Bahia, Brazil.
Drs. Janet and Willis Reed

At the weekly stock fair in Punata, Bolivia, ranchers and their families gather to buy and sell cattle.

Carlos D. Conde, Inter-American Development Bank

An aerial view of the Guayaquil, Ecuador, slum where about 250,000 people live in shacks, many of them built on stilts over the river.

critical import. In 1982, Honduras experienced a 1.5 percent decline in economic growth while the population increased 3 percent and unemployment reached 20 percent. The country is sliding backwards, and there is little investment from abroad.

Most of the money provided by aid programs is apparently skimmed off through top-level government corruption. One diplomat in Central America was quoted as saying that the aid comes into Honduras and goes right back out to Miami. Corruption of this sort is not unique to Honduras; high government officials simply pick up any funds available and send them to banks in Miami instead of investing them in the Honduran economy.

Representative Gerry E. Studds, congressman from Massachusetts has reported that Honduras is not a good place in which to be sick and hungry. He and two other congressional representatives visited health and nutrition centers in the rural areas of Honduras in late 1980. There, in Studds's words, they "saw tiny children whose diets have condemned them already to die." Honduran government officials have said that their country will need one-half billion dollars a year in American aid for twelve years, a total of $6 billion, in order to pull out of its depressed state. Honduras now receives $101 million a year in United States aid; it is hardly likely that more will be appropriated. A question to be asked is where does the money go? Who would get the proposed $6 billion? The poor, or the banks in Miami?

El Salvador is a similar case. It has a population of about 5.2 million, which is expected to double by

2005. While its predicament is basically no different from that of Guatemala or Honduras, it is, in fact, more alarming. El Salvador is about the size of the state of Massachusetts and has a population density of some 570 per square mile. Up to 70 percent of its people live in rural areas and about 41 percent of the labor force is engaged in agriculture. With a per capita income of about $636, El Salvador cannot afford such an increase in its population.

Here again, 5 percent of the population accounts for 38 percent of the national income. In El Salvador 85 percent of all houses lack electricity, running water, and adequate sanitation. Life expectancy is about sixty-two years, and malnutrition is rampant among children. Diarrhea, often an indication of a more serious illness, is so common among the poor that they ignore it. Often children are brought to a clinic only when an illness is too far advanced to cure. Usually the families cannot spare the time to seek medical aid for themselves or their children; work and immediate survival come first.

The average level of literacy in the cities of these three countries is 56 percent; in rural areas it is always much lower.

South America, a Mixed Case

South America has both urban and rural nations. While there are similarities between countries, there are also differences in population makeup and economic conditions among them.

In Ecuador, Bolivia, and Paraguay 45 percent of the population is still engaged in agriculture. These people have low income per person, high infant mortality, and high population growth. Peru has these same problems, but it is becoming highly urbanized, with almost 70 percent of its people now living in cities and towns. There is little industry in the land, and commerce and the government (including the military) provide employment for the greater part of the growing urban middle class. Unequal distribution of wealth is evident: the annual average income in 1981 was $1,122, but many of the Indians in the mountains live on a barter economy.

The urbanized nations of South America can give a more satisfactory accounting of their populations, at least on the surface. Uruguay, for instance, has a slower population growth. Though it is no bigger than the state of Washington and its main occupation is in the meat and meat processing industries, it has a development similar to that of the larger, more industrialized countries—Argentina, Brazil, Chile, Colombia, and Venezuela.

Argentina is noteworthy in that it developed its population through immigration. From 1856 to 1930 it admitted some 6.5 million immigrants. Almost half were Italians; most of the others were Spanish, French, and Germans. About 90 percent of those immigrants settled in the Buenos Aires metropolitan area, the remainder generally in other large cities. After 1952, immigration essentially ceased, but the ethnically mixed population was by then long established. Argentina became an urban nation—79 percent of its people live in cities—with a large middle class and labor force.

Chile also followed a pattern of urban development (82.6 percent), but with no immigration to speak of.

Brazil has fewer urban people (68 percent), but it has gone to great lengths in the last fifteen years to lay down an industrialized base. Brazil has the highest population in South America (128 million), and it threatens to double by 2012.

Both Brazil and Chile have high per capita incomes—$2,214 and $2,560 respectively—with Argentina remaining far behind at $966. All of them, however, rank with the poorer countries where low life expectancy is concerned. This reflects the urban development problems that are characteristic of Latin American cities: excessive growth of slum areas that breed disease among ill-fed, ill-housed people.

Mushroom Cities

They rise like mushrooms, almost overnight. They are built out of the most ephemeral materials— shacks made of cardboard boxes and plastic sheets. The people live there crowded together; ten to seventeen children and grownups often occupy an area of thirty or forty square feet. Garbage, including human waste, is everywhere, strewn in the narrow alleyways, and there is no running water. It is impossible to stay clean and healthy in such conditions. These slums are called by various names: the *villas miserias* in Buenos Aires, the *barriadas* in Lima, *tugurios* in Bogotá and Medellín in Colombia, and *favelas* in Rio de Janeiro and other Brazilian cities. But they are essentially no different from one another, and the health and social problems are the same everywhere. Some of the worst slums in Central America are in Panama City and Colón in Panama.

Aina Bergval was assistant information officer of UNICEF in Guatemala City in 1979 when she wrote in a technical journal about David "The Thief." David was fourteen and lived in the poorest section of Panama City with his mother and younger sisters. His mother did laundry for a living and drank heavily, and a man lived with them who had no steady work. David's father had abandoned them and gone to live in Colón where he started a new family. David was arrested twice by the police for stealing. He had more than one excuse for stealing. One was that he wanted to buy his father a present; another was that the man who lived with him told him to get some money; another was that he was hungry. Are such children criminals?

When social workers asked children like David what they would appreciate most in their lives, the answers were hardly those of hardened criminals: tenderness, happy parents, a job for their fathers, a new home, eating well every day, and no need to go to Juvenile Court for help again. The slum is the criminal, the lives of its inhabitants no more valuable than the garbage that rots in the sun.

Land as Wealth

Why do such slums exist? The *campesinos* (rural peasants) find it difficult to make a living from the land and mistakenly think they and their families will find relief in the city. They have no trade; they are illiterate; and they will have to compete with many others like themselves for the few unskilled jobs available in the city. In the country the peasants' connection to the land is weak at best. Most of them are tenant farmers or itinerant farmhands, picking up work during the harvest or planting season. The city is their last hope, but they gain nothing by the move. If they go back to being itinerant farmhands they will go with the slum as their base.

In Chile and Brazil 2 percent of the population are reported to possess 50 percent of the arable land. In Venezuela 3 percent own or control 90 percent. In 1968 the ruling families of El Salvador, said to number fourteen, owned 95 percent of the land. In general, outside Mexico, 5 percent of the population of Latin America owns half the land.

If conditions in Latin America are to improve, land reform is crucial, not only to help the *campesinos* earn a decent living, but to give them a sense of participation in the development of their country. In El Salvador land reform has become so important that people have killed to prevent it; and it has also become a measure by which to judge the sincerity of the commitment of the ruling classes to change the whole structure of society.

The Salvadoran Example

On March 6, 1980, a new reform government in El Salvador announced its Basic Agrarian Reform Law. By May 1980, three phases had been published all together. The total acreage involved covered about 50 percent of all farmland in the country and affected some 200,000 *campesino* families.

The objective of this law was to give the peasants title to a specific number of acres, either through cooperative or individual ownership. For instance, in Phase I the government took over about three hundred farms comprising some 518,000 acres (15 percent of all farmland). This land was given to peasant cooperatives. Control was to pass from 242 wealthy families to 60,000 or 70,000 poor families. Compensation to the former landowners was handled through a government agency called the Salvadoran Institute for Agrarian Reform (ISTA). ISTA actually owned each farm, supposedly until the cooperative members learned to manage it themselves. However, nothing definite was stated about when they would become owners.

In the beginning many of the peasants had no idea what their role was to be, and the government did not encourage them to participate in the running of the farms. By this time the reform government had vanished, and a more conservative regime held power. On many of the old haciendas, or large farms, the same managers were retained to ensure continued production. Some *campesinos* saw only one *patrón* (the former landowner) supplanted by another (the government). As of early 1984, reports by the United States government and American labor advisers, both of whom monitored and gave aid to the programs, were not good. The cooperatives had severe money problems, management was weak, there was a surplus of workers, and they were accumulating large debts. Only about a third of the cooperatives were reported to be doing well.

In another phase, renters and sharecroppers were allowed to apply for ownership of land they were tilling. Landowners, however, threatened to throw them off the land if they did so. Thousands were actually driven off the land before they could apply for ownership. Landowners could then claim that no one was using the land, and assert their own right to retain it.

Those who work to enforce the land reform program have a dangerous job. The car of one union leader has been machine-gunned; others have received threats. One received an envelope containing ashes, which symbolize death. There have been many assassinations. In fact, by the end of 1981 about ninety-two members of one farmers' group, the Salvadoran Communal Union (UCS), were murdered by the armed forces of the government and by private groups working in collusion with the soldiers. The first head of ISTA, José Rodolfo Viera, was among those who were killed.

Phase III was supposed to last until the end of 1983. A new, conservative Constituent Assembly was elected in March 1982. The Assembly intended to let Phase III lapse in spite of the many abuses connected with its operation. The UCS, which claims forty thousand members, warned the Assembly that its members would not react kindly to such maneuvers. "If you have five thousand beneficiaries and they lose out," one leader said, "they get frustrated, and that's five thousand machine guns that will turn against the government." While the statement is an exaggeration, it is still more than an idle threat. The Assembly took the hint and voted to extend Phase III until June 30, 1984, thereby giving the peasants more time to buy their land. However, the landowners' threats continued to be translated into action by death squads.

This land reform, with all its setbacks and frustrations, is the most extensive ever attempted in a Latin American country. The example does not give land reformists in other countries much encouragement. There are people in El Salvador who want it to succeed, however. One of these is José Napoleón Duarte, elected president of the country in May 1984. He faces formidable opposition to his plans to reform the country, but he has the backing of the United States government and the people of El Salvador who voted him into office.

Empty Pockets, Empty Stomachs

Today in Latin America it is not only the poor who are under duress. Since 1982 a severe worldwide depression has been particularly hard on the middle strata of society, both blue-collar and white-collar workers. They have been reduced to Third World status in many places.

These middle strata in Latin America cover a wide area of occupations: owners of small and middle-sized farms, skilled workers, public employees, and many different types of salaried or self-employed professionals. Their family life and homes are more stable than those of the poor, fathers and husbands are not likely to abandon their wives and children. They usually have more education, the wife may work as well as the husband, and they have access to medical care.

In the past the middle strata have shown few liberal tendencies, often joining with the conservative ruling elements to maintain an economic status quo—that is, to keep the poor repressed. It was in their interest to do so, they believed.

Argentina, Brazil, Chile, Colombia, Venezuela, Costa Rica, Mexico, almost every country in Latin America is now faced with the momentous new problem of repaying a huge foreign debt accumulated over the last several decades. The urbanized countries all borrowed heavily from foreign banks and governments in order to develop new industry or build an infrastructure to encourage such development. There were also numerous imports of high-cost consumer products that the upper and middle classes wanted. The governments, in other words, allowed more imports to come in than they could pay for. When the economy was good, the debt was of no consequence. Some governments satisfied internal needs by printing more money, a practice that is still followed in some nations and that only increases inflation. In Argentina and Brazil, demands for raises by labor unions were usually met. In Brazil an index was created whereby the wages of all workers, government and civilian, automatically increased to meet inflation. It became an endless cycle. As an Argentine worker said some years ago, "My paycheck goes up the stairway while inflation takes the escalator." Inflation in Argentina is reported to have been almost 600 percent in 1983; in Brazil, 200 percent. Money was becoming literally worthless.

The agrarian countries face the same problems. In the past they, too, imported more than they could pay for and looked for foreign credits from the sale of their one or two export crops. Demand for these has dropped as well as their price on the world market. They also borrowed from foreign banks to finance their own internal projects. Now they must continue to import many products, such as petroleum and machine parts, just to keep going. Although Ecuador is a major oil-exporting nation, it finds itself in the same situation, with a foreign debt of over $6 billion.

Latin American countries have no foreign currency available with which to pay their huge foreign debts. There is high unemployment at home, and exports are all down because other countries cannot afford to buy what the Latin Americans are offering for sale. Brazil now owes foreign banks about $90 billion, an astronomical sum—the largest debt, in fact, of all Third World countries. Brazil is having trouble just meeting the interest payments on its debt. Argentina owes some $40 billion, Chile about $17 million, and they both have the same problem of repayment. Even little Costa Rica owes almost $3 billion and labors under 65 percent inflation with unemployment at about 15 percent.

These countries have turned to the International

Monetary Fund (IMF) for loans in order to make their interest payments. The IMF, a bank set up by contributions from 146 nations, helps governments cover their foreign debts by "quick-fix" loans, thereby allowing the nations to maintain financial stability and credit throughout the world.

There is a price for these loans, however. The IMF has been telling Latin American countries how to run their economies so as to ensure that their debts will in fact be reduced. The bank has forced Argentina, Brazil, and Chile to cut back on expenses: automatic raises to workers must be reduced, as well as imports, for instance. These actions have created hardships in the countries, especially among the middle strata, leading to strikes and riots. There have also been demands that the governments resign and that the foreign debts be repudiated. Some of the governments have had to declare a moratorium on debt payments until they can get their chaotic financial situations straightened out. The IMF has resisted such decisions, and several financial confrontations have resulted.

The Third World Widens

Such conditions, coupled with internal pressures, have caused the poor and some members of the middle strata to combine forces at times. Sometimes their leaders meet in the political arena. Sometimes the people gather in the mountains to train as guerrillas, intent on overthrowing the harsh regimes under which they live. This is now happening most visibly in Central America. The regimes there have been dominated by the *caudillo* and the military tradition of Latin America, formidable opponents to any program that seeks to alleviate the sufferings of the Third World. In South America, at the moment, the country that promises the best recovery from internal repression is Argentina. But the new government treads a narrow path between its authoritarian history and its democratic future. The foreign debt does not help.

Strongmen and Generals

Military power in Latin America is power.
—**Nicaraguan anti-Sandinista guerrilla**

Every country in Latin America has had a strong-man or general as leader at one time or another. In South America, discounting Suriname and Guyana, by the end of 1984 only Chile and Paraguay were under the control of military regimes. Brazil and Uruguay were in the process of giving control back to civilians. In 1983, however, six countries were under military control: Chile, Paraguay, Brazil, Uruguay, Argentina, and Bolivia. Although these countries seem to be making progress toward more democratic systems, the threat of military intervention is always present. Indeed, the belief that "military power in Latin America is power" is a deeply ingrained tradition. A look at the ABCs of South America—Argentina, Brazil, and Chile—will provide an illustration of the nature of these military strongmen and what they did and did not accomplish.

Argentina
The Heir to Mussolini

On June 4, 1943, during World War II, Colonel Juan Domingo Perón, together with a circle of pro-German military officers, carried out a coup in which they overthrew the president of Argentina. Perón was a career military officer, trained in the German tradition, and a great admirer of Benito Mussolini, the dictator of Italy. Perón and his followers believed Argentina had to be industrialized, had to come out of its semicolonial status, and had to stop relying on just a few export products for its national wealth. Perón believed he could unite the different interests in the country by preaching his belief in a "Great Argentina," destined to take its place as the leading nation of South America. His intention was to follow the pattern of Mussolini.

By 1944, Perón was vice-president, minister of war, and secretary of labor and social welfare. This combination of powerful government posts helped him keep his eye on both the army and the government, and at the same time put him in close touch with the working class.

Perón began developing a new following outside the military. He talked with people who were out of work, who had no money to pay the rent, or who were hungry, and then he personally helped them. He also backed the demands of unions for pay raises and better working conditions, demands that had been largely ignored up to then. In short, Perón soon built a strong political base among the working class, especially the labor unions. No other politician had so courted them or been so aware of their potential power. Others dismissed these workers contemptuously as the *descamisados*, the shirtless ones. Perón took up the name and made it a title to be proud of. The *descamisados* were his people, and he meant to lead them.

Also in 1944, Perón met a woman who was destined to become even more of a symbol of success and hope for the working class than Perón himself. Her name was Eva Duarte. Born of a poor family, she had a driving ambition to succeed. She had started out as an actress, but after she and Perón met, she moved on to higher objectives. She became his wife, and for all intents and purposes she ran the country with him. She held no public office, but was closely involved in all of Perón's activities including blatant corruption, until her death in 1952. Today, Evita, as she was lovingly called by her followers, is still revered in Argentina.

By 1945, Perón was becoming so powerful that the army began to fear him. He had created a new force in Latin America, the organized working class, and the generals did not like any challenges to their power. When Perón felt the army was dictating to him, he suddenly resigned his government posts and went into seclusion. The generals took over the government and quickly arrested Perón, putting him in prison. The military, however, had not recognized the power of Evita. She quickly roused his loyal unions, and soon the streets of Buenos Aires were packed with Peronistas demanding the return of their leader. Perón was released and appeared on the balcony of the Casa Rosada, the presidential palace, where he announced his resignation from the army and told the shouting throng that he would run for the presidency. Perón won the presidency in February 1945 and began a rule that ended ten years later, in 1955. Ironically, Perón's election in 1945 was honest, not something always to be taken for granted in Latin America. His *descamisados* were the mainstay of his support.

Once in office, Perón proved true to the predictions of his enemies. He had not said in so many words that he would create a totalitarian state—that is, one under the complete control of the government—but he set about doing just that. He allowed only Peronista labor unions to function; he closed the universities or made them conform to the government's dictates; he put business and industry under tight controls, and he censored newspapers or closed them down if they printed stories or articles without government approval. The Argentine Congress became packed with Perón's supporters. Thousands of opponents to his authority were imprisoned or exiled; some were beaten, tortured, or murdered.

By 1955 Perón had put Argentina deep into foreign debt by using government funds to finance grandiose projects, without giving business, industry, and agriculture an opportunity to develop. In other words, no earnings were generated to pay for the projects. Even his working-class following temporarily deteriorated as inflation grew and the money they earned bought less and less. The Catholic hierarchy turned against him, to the point where he was finally excommunicated for arresting some bishops. His morally corrupt private life added to the church's disapproval of him. Finally, there were enough factions in the armed forces that opposed his policies so that a coup was planned. In September 1955 Perón was thrown out of office and shortly thereafter out of Argentina. He made his way through several countries in Latin America and finally settled in Spain.

Absent but Present

Argentina got rid of Perón, but it did not get rid of his influence. The labor unions remained powerful, and through them the Peronistas played a significant role in all elections, even though they were not allowed to function as a political party. The generals tried to wipe out all traces of Perón and his influence, but Perón remained the idol of the working class. He was able to command his followers from abroad, and at his direction they voted for those candidates who favored a Peronist policy.

The military, especially the army, the strongest force, feared not only the Peronistas but the communists as well. The military watched over every elected government, taking over whenever they were dissatisfied. As a result, there was little continuity in government, and Argentina's problems only worsened as divisions increased. The economy never really recovered its high position of the early 1950s, and inflation kept growing.

The communists and socialists in a bid for power also tried to adopt some of Perón's policies and claim them for their own. The Peronistas resented this, and the two sides attacked each other. Opponents took to the streets, and soon arguments gave way to gun battles, kidnappings, and murder.

By 1972, the situation in Argentina was so bad that the military gave in and allowed Perón to return from exile. They expected him to back the conservative faction of his followers and thereby provide some stability to Argentine society, which was now badly fractured. In 1973, he was again elected to the presidency, receiving 62 percent of the vote. The large vote represented a desperate hope on the part of the population for peace and a return to the happy days of Perón's first years as president. The working class regarded his name as unassailable, in spite of his corruption, civil and human rights violations, and the economic disasters he had imposed on the country.

But by 1974, at the age of seventy-eight, Perón had run out of time: he died in July of that year. He was succeeded by his third wife, Isabel Martínez de Perón, a former dancer whom he had married in Spain and who had been legally elected vice-president in 1973. She was no Evita, however, and her government has been referred to as a farce, even a black comedy. She could not control members of her government, there was more than the usual corruption, and the economy was in deep trouble with inflation rising. She had no control over the old forces that had returned to the streets where open guerrilla warfare had resumed.

In 1976, the military again stepped in, Isabel was overthrown and subsequently convicted of depositing $740,000 in charity funds in her personal bank account. She was kept under house arrest for five years and then allowed to leave the country in 1981.

Repression and Disaster

If Isabel's rule was a black comedy, then what followed is a black mark on the conscience of the Argentine people. After the generals toppled Isabel, they turned their attention to purging the country of leftists and terrorists who, they claimed, were running riot and threatening the democratic institutions of Argentina. Indeed, the guerrilla movement had gotten out of hand and was fast becoming a state within a state. There were an estimated ten thousand Argentines in the movement, and they had built up an operating fund of $150 million, mostly through bank robberies and kidnappings.

The bloodbath that followed, however, was many times worse than the situation warranted and was hardly conducive to protecting democratic institutions. Thousands of people were arrested, held without trial or charges, beaten, tortured, and sometimes killed. Much of the killing was done by death squads operating in collusion with the government and armed forces. Still unexplained is the fate of at least six thousand—some claim many more—*desaparecidos* (the "disappeared") who were arrested or kidnapped and never heard from again. The military instituted its own brand of terrorism in place of an earlier one; now, in fact, terrorism became a policy of the state. The majority of Argentines became quiet, cowed by this official threat.

No one knows how long the situation would have lasted had it not been for a disastrous military adventure undertaken by the ruling junta. In 1982, the Argentine rulers decided to invade the British-held Falkland Islands, known as the Islas Malvinas in Latin America, located about 250 miles off the southern coast and long claimed by Argentina.

The Argentines won a few victories, but the British commandos soon overran the force stationed there, reconquering the island in about ten weeks. Lieutenant General Leopoldo Galtieri, the Argentine president, and his cohorts were removed from power, and the new president, Major General Reynaldo Bignone, soon announced plans to return the government to civilian rule. The military junta's effort to regain the confidence of the Argentine people had turned into a terrible defeat; the military leaders were humiliated and could not continue in power.

A New Start

Immediately the Peronist party returned to the front, claiming to represent the populace, particularly the working class. However, the party comprised factions of widely different political views, and it knew that it would have to unite these factions before it could unify the country. The main opposition to the Peronists was the old, mildly socialist Radical party, founded in the 1890s and itself divided into two factions. The ruling junta allowed fifteen parties to run for office, excluding the communists. The Peronist party, which claimed to be sure of some 30 percent of the vote, held the greatest promise of victory. In spite of the attempts by the military to eliminate the Peronists and the causes for their existence, Argentina seemed to remain devoted to the memory of its famous son and his principles.

To the astonishment of the Peronists and the world, however, they lost the election held on October 30, 1983. The winner was Raúl Alfonsin, fifty-six years old, of the Radical party. Alfonsin had always championed human rights, even in Argentina's blackest hours, and he had accused both the Peronists and the military of bringing the country to ruin. A majority of the voters agreed with him— 52 percent to be exact, an extraordinary victory. A demoralized junta passed the reins of government to Alfonsin on December 10, 1983, two months ahead of schedule.

Cleaning Up

Just before the ruling junta left office, it issued a decree of amnesty for the military, pardoning all crimes the army had committed during the antiterrorist campaign that started in 1976. This maneuver could not go unopposed; many families in Argentina were demanding justice for the murder of their relatives. Within two weeks after taking office, Alfonsin and the new Argentine Congress repealed the amnesty law. Alfonsin forced more than half the generals and two-thirds of the admirals to retire. Then he made himself commander-in-chief of the armed forces and removed internal security from military control. He also set about prosecuting former junta members for their roles in the anti-terrorist campaign and formed a commission to investigate the fate of the six thousand or more *desaparecidos*. Mass graves began to turn up soon after Alfonsin took office, and the cries for justice increased. To offset any plans the military might have about a coup, he appointed his own people to vacant military posts; many of these men were young, reform-minded officers.

Alfonsin also moved to reform the Peronista unions. They and the Peronist party had worked hand-in-glove for years. After 1976, the generals had taken over the unions, but later relinquished control, giving them back to the old leaders. Alfonsin asked Congress to decree new elections to cleanse the unions of their long rule by suspect Peronist leaders. That and the fact that he did not provide a sufficient wage increase to meet the high rate of inflation raised the hackles of Peronist union and party leaders, and the Peronist-dominated Congress rejected his request. The confrontations between the opposition and Alfonsin's government became so heated that they threatened the frail peace in the country. This led to negotiations between the Peronists, other parties, and Alfonsin, and those talks resulted in a signed agreement on how to deal with national issues. Isabel Perón returned from Spain to encourage and participate in the agreement.

Alfonsin must also deal with Argentina's foreign debt, which totaled about $45 billion in mid-1984. This problem may ultimately be his most difficult, for it cannot be changed by simply passing a law and it is tied in closely with wages and salaries in Argentina. The interest alone on the debt, which was due in 1984, amounts to a couple of billion dollars. Almost 55 percent of foreign earnings must go toward payments on debt; that means no meaningful wage increases for workers. Whether the unions will continue to accept inadequate wages in the name of paying off the debt remains to be seen.

The past works against all the good intentions of Raúl Alfonsin. In fifty-three years, only one Argentine leader—Juan Perón—finished his duly elected term in office. All other presidents in this period, including Perón after his second election, have been overthrown. At the moment, the majority of the Argentine people are behind Alfonsin's efforts to put Argentina on the road to democracy and economic recovery. But should the military regain its confidence, or the Peronists decide not to cooperate with the government, Alfonsin may find himself in trouble.

Brazil
Life and History

On August 24, 1954, Getúlio Vargas, then the elected president of Brazil, committed suicide. The country's generals had asked for his resignation. Assassination and large-scale corruption in the Vargas government had been uncovered, though Vargas himself appears to have been honest. The country was also in a grave economic crisis, and Vargas had not been able to provide the leadership necessary to solve Brazil's problems. He was seventy-one years old and had been either president or dictator of Brazil for all but five years since 1930. The country was getting tired of him, and the generals had the backing of the people.

Vargas left a letter, his last testament, to the Brazilian people. He had aligned himself with them, he said, but could no longer prevent the forces of repression from overwhelming the country. He died for the freedom of Brazil, adding that he "serenely" took the "first step on the road to eternity" and now entered history. Vargas was a strongman with his eye on immortality.

In Brazil, Getúlio Vargas was the first charismatic leader to rise to national prominence. He was installed as president in 1930 by the military after an attempt had been made to deprive him of an election victory. Vargas came from the state of Rio Grande do Sul, a land of gauchos, large landowners, and the rule of the gun. He grew up under a governor who believed his authority should prevail over any congressional conclave. In Rio de Janeiro, Vargas emulated that governor and gradually took power into his own hands, finally becoming dictator.

Vargas was responsible for unifying the country, introducing much needed social and labor legislation, encouraging the growth of labor unions, and developing industry. During most of his time in the presidency he was backed by the armed forces and held control of the Congress and provincial governors. Without a strong leader in those years the country probably would have committed political suicide and degenerated into provincial republics.

Vargas was the man who brought the country together.

Vargas ruled until 1945, when the military removed him. Brazil had taken part in the fight against Hitler and Mussolini, and at the end of the war there was a deep desire for change in the country. Vargas tried to oppose the movement but he lost.

Between 1945 and 1950, Brazil was run by a lackluster elected president, General Enrico Gaspar Dutra, who had been Vargas's war minister. The country's economic situation deteriorated under Dutra. Inflation grew, and workers began dreaming of the good old days under Vargas. In 1950, Vargas ran again for the presidency and was returned to power. But his administration as a duly elected president was a disaster. His years as a dictator had defeated him; he could not operate in a democratic framework. He had united the country, but he could not keep it united.

Although Vargas entered history without fear, it is difficult to say exactly how history will judge him. Certainly his life was in the mode of those Latin American strongmen who force change on their countries. Sometimes that change is beneficial; sometimes it is disastrous. And usually the changes are economic rather than social or political.

From 1954 to 1964, after Vargas, civilians ruled the government of Brazil. The country continued to face the same unresolved problems of inflation and rising foreign debt. In 1961, João Goulart was elected president. When he appeared to be organizing the lower classes, including peasants and workers, against the established power structure of business, landowners, and the military, he was removed from office by a coup. The military has remained in power ever since. The current president, General João Baptista Figueiredo, although retired from the army, is the fifth general to occupy the post since 1964. There is a constitutional front to the government, for the president is nominally elected by a 686-member electoral college, many of whose members are representatives to the national Congress. The fact is, however, that since 1964 the candidate has always been chosen by a committee of military officers and then elected by the college. Thus, there has been some maneuvering in the process by officers seeking the presidency, but it can hardly be called a democratic process.

When the junta took over in 1964, it used stringent measures, including torture, but succeeding presidents have moved away from such extremes. Figueiredo has announced a return to civilian government, and political parties have been allowed to function once more. In March 1983, elections were held for state governors, and even though some of those elected are distasteful to the generals, they have been allowed to stay in office, and Figueiredo has continued to permit free elections.

One new governor is a socialist named Leonel Brizola, who now runs the state of Rio de Janeiro. He was exiled by the junta in the past and is now wary of how he conducts himself. A firebrand in the 1950s and 1960s, he is much mellower today and views the armed forces as "a kind of skeleton that keeps the national organism on its feet." There is no other element in the country that holds such a historical position, Brizola claims. Such statements, especially by a socialist, must surely make the generals feel more at ease. They are understandably anxious to avoid attempts to bring the military to justice for past acts, as is happening in Argentina, where civilians are returning to power.

Brazil has suffered along with all Third World countries from radical increases in oil prices since 1973. It also made overly ambitious attempts to industrialize its rural economy, and the depression of 1980–81 left it stranded with high unemployment and a foreign debt amounting to $93 billion. President Figueiredo, in an attempt to satisfy the IMF, reduced automatic raises from 100 percent to 80 percent of inflation. This did not make the working people of Brazil any happier with their plight; there have been numerous demonstrations, not all of them peaceable. The revival of political parties has also provided the opposition with a chance to voice its discontent. Then the populace started agitating for election of the next president by popular vote, thereby taking the election out of the politically suspect electoral college. These demands show the desire of the people of Brazil to have a say in their future immediately, not according to the slower schedule envisaged by the ruling generals.

Brazil entered 1984 with both hope and anxiety. The questions still remain: Will Vargas and the generals who came after him go down in history as skeletons to be buried once and for all? And will the next leaders stabilize the country and preserve its traditions? Only time and current efforts to initiate a democratic process will tell.

Chile

From 1927 to 1931, Chile was ruled by Carlos Ibáñez, a man who rejected democracy. Like Vargas in Brazil, he established certain reforms that aided labor and provided for social welfare but denied any political freedom to the country. After Ibáñez was removed from office, a series of political parties, running from left to right, established and maintained civilian rule. Even more surprising, there were no assassinations or attempted revolutions or coups. All elections, from national offices down to local positions, were contested only through the ballot box. Chile seemed to have achieved political stability.

But the stability was only on the surface. Social inequalities continued, resulting in economic hardships. The big landowners continued to exert control over their workers, even to the point of determining their vote. With low wages and little hope of change, the peasants fled to the cities, where they gathered in slums. Unemployment grew as Chilean industry was unable to absorb the growing urban labor pool. The Christian Democratic party, based on Catholic social doctrines, promised much but delivered little. At the same time, the communists were promising to redistribute land and wealth, nationalize foreign-owned industry, and allow greater participation in government by workers and peasants.

Salvador Allende Gossens, a Marxist, had run for the presidency twice and lost, in 1952 and 1958. In 1970, he ran again, this time under the Unidad Popular (Popular Unity) label, a combination of Marxist, radical, and small-party groups. The UP won by a small plurality, and for the first time in Latin American history a Marxist was legally elected to the office of president. But Allende had too many forces arrayed against him. In the first place, he did not have a majority of the people behind him. Then he moved to nationalize many businesses (have the government own and run them). This created greater dissatisfaction among those who favored private enterprise; the non-socialist liberals, the conservatives, and the business community of Chile became less and less willing to cooperate.

The United States government and American financial interests in Chile were against Allende; our government withheld much-needed economic aid to the country and at the same time gave secret financial help to Allende's enemies. The plan was to "destabilize" the Chilean government—a euphemism for overthrowing Allende. Allende's major opponents saw not just a badly run government but also the threat of a communist state being established in South America. Chile had become the scene of an international crisis in the United States–Soviet ideological war.

Allende became more and more isolated as one group after another turned against him. Even the communists disagreed with him: they felt he had not been radical enough in his efforts to build socialism in Chile. The Chilean Congress would not pass the legislation he requested. Shortages became more common, strikes occurred more frequently, and by the summer of 1973 the country was almost at a standstill. In August the Congress called in the generals, and that spelled the end of whatever democracy Chile had enjoyed. On September 11 a fierce battle began, in the course of which the army attacked and bombed the presidential palace. Allende and a few of his close followers died while defending themselves against overwhelming odds. The military announced that he had commited suicide, but subsequent events make that claim questionable.

Cleaning Up

The generals then "cleansed" the country of all "leftist" elements. It is estimated that in the weeks that followed the coup, some 25,000 Chileans were slaughtered by the new military regime, and perhaps 100,000 were sent to prisons and concentration camps where many of them were tortured and murdered. Bodies were dumped into rivers, which literally ran red with blood. The Chilean military junta then imposed a repressive government on the people, wiping out all civil liberties and eliminating all political activity. These actions were a direct violation of the Chilean constitution, passed in 1925, a fact that did not deter the junta from its work. Like Argentina after 1976, Chile became a quiet, depressed land.

The man appointed to rule Chile was General Augusto Pinochet Ugarte, a dour, no-nonsense dictator who has pursued his "communist" enemies ruthlessly. His repressive arm is DINA, the National Department of Intelligence. Its tentacles have even penetrated into Washington, D.C., where his agents assassinated Allende's former foreign minister in 1976. An American and former CIA trainer who spent fifteen years in Chile, Michael Vernon Townley, confessed to the crime and implicated three members of DINA, one a military colleague of Pinochet and former head of DINA. All suspects remain free in Chile and will not be extradited to the United States, at least not by the Pinochet regime.

In 1980, Pinochet submitted a new constitution to a vote of the Chilean people. Although the vote, called a plebiscite, was favorable, there had been no popular participation in drawing up the constitution. Along with the approval was a stipulation that Pinochet continue as president until 1989. Since 1980, however, the economic situation in Chile has become bleak, with a large foreign debt and high unemployment. The people no longer favor the generals as they did in 1973. A series of monthly demonstrations in 1983 nearly turned into open warfare between the people and Pinochet's regime. About forty people were killed. There has even been a growing Allende cult. Maybe, some think, he was not so wrong after all.

In an anniversary speech on September 11, 1983, Pinochet portrayed himself as the savior of the country. He said he had removed the "tragic Marxist experiment that sought to impose a totalitarian system in our land." In its place his government had presented "a new system, full of humanism and with a clear democratic character." This statement came from a man who was instrumental in purging all social institutions of any worth, who has imposed a draconian rule on citizens and refuses to recognize the growing civilian discontent with his government.

Change and No Change

Other countries in South America share a history similar to that of Argentina, Brazil, and Chile. Paraguay, for example, has been under tight control of a military *caudillo* since 1954. In that year, General Alfredo Stroessner led a successful coup and has been happily elected president at every "election" since. His is probably the most efficient dictatorship in South America. Uruguay has lived under a military regime since 1973. The generals finally gave way, however, and in elections held in November 1984, a moderate politician, Julio Maria Sanguinetti, was elected president. He is scheduled to take office on March 1, 1985, and he seeks to form a govenment of "national understanding."

The new democratic government in Argentina is making its neighbors—Paraguay and Chile—very nervous. Argentina is becoming a meeting ground for exiles and offers proof that generals can be relegated to a limited role in government. Undoubtedly the dictators will only intensify their repressive systems in order to keep out the winds of change.

Bolivia has had a change of government, on the average, more than once a year since independence in 1824. In 1980 a military coup again changed the government. Blatant corruption (including military control of the lucrative drug trade) and economic decline became so bad that in 1982 a series of nationwide strikes brought the country to a halt. The military leaders conceded defeat and turned the government back to the civilians who had been legally elected in 1980.

The winner in that 1980 election, Hernán Siles Zuazo, heads the Democratic and Popular Unity party, a coalition of communists and less radical democrats. He and his government need the cooperation of the Bolivian Congress and the labor unions in order to rebuild the shattered economy, with a foreign debt estimated to be between $2.5 and $4.4 billion and an annual inflation rate of 1,500 percent. Not much hope was given for this government, but in spite of strikes and the kidnapping of the president by conservative officers, as of the end of 1984 it was still active. Countries such as Peru, Venezuela, and Colombia, as well as the United States, reacted against the kidnapping and warned that Bolivia would be isolated if the officers took over. However, the internal situation in Bolivia remains very unstable, and there is no telling what may happen in the immediate future.

Central America

Central American countries have gone through crises similar to those in South America. Except for Costa Rica, however, there have been few democratic experiments. The only stable rule seems to have rested in the military and the *caudillo*, with the usual dangerous consequences. While this region suffers from the same economic problems as South America, social and political questions are the main issues of contention. These issues have their roots in the effects of long authoritarian rule. El Salvador and Guatelmala are typical of the struggle to resolve these questions. El Salvador has been in the throes of a civil war for about five years; Guatemala is peaceful on the surface, but the embers of revolt are there, waiting only for the right wind to inflame them.

El Salvador
La Matanza Continues

On a hot July day in 1975 in San Salvador, the capital of El Salvador, a group of university students registered a protest. In a land of hunger and poverty, the students resented the government's allocation of $3.5 million for the Miss Universe contest. Such an amount of money would buy seed, farm implements, hospital supplies, food—the list of needs was endless.

While the demonstrators were crossing a bridge, soldiers opened fire on them. The students scattered, most jumping off the bridge into an abandoned roadway below. But there was no escape that way, for members of the National Guard and the police were waiting for them. As the students tried to flee, they were shot at and sliced with machetes. Even rescue workers from a nearby hospital were attacked when they tried to aid the wounded. After the bloodletting, the count was twelve students killed, eighty wounded, and twenty-four "unaccounted for," who had joined the "disappeared" along with their counterparts in Argentina and Chile.

This attack was not an unusual occurrence. The repressive nature of the government's armed forces has long been a reality in Salvadoran society. The military comprises four branches that are run separately but work quite effectively together. They are the army, national guard, treasury police, and national police. One military academy in El Salvador conveniently supplies senior officers for all four branches.

There are also paramilitary right-wing death squads that have been responsible for secret acts of terror that include kidnappings, torture, and assassinations. The government has always denied statements by some Salvadoran officials and civilians that conservative military officers ran the death squads. As of mid-1984, however, no members of any death squad had ever been arrested. One of those accused was Colonel Nicolás Carranza, chief of the treasury police; another was Roberto d'Aubuisson, an ex–army intelligence major. Both men have denied the accusations. One of the death squads is named the Maximiliano Hernández Martínez Anti-Communist Brigade.

In January 1932 General Maximiliano Hernández Martínez suppressed a revolt of poor peasants in western El Salvador. He did it with such efficiency that estimates of the number of people killed run up to 30,000. The killing is still known as La Matanza (The Massacre). The reasons for the revolt are familiar in Latin American history: a subsistence-level standard of living among peasants and Indians, and harsh treatment by landowners and officials. Communists in El Salvador had encouraged the revolt and led part of it, but it could hardly be called an international conspiracy.

General Martínez also turned his attention to the government and in the same year engineered a coup that put him in power for twelve years. After him generals continued to occupy the presidency and fraudulent elections were commonplace. It is no wonder that a right-wing death squad should look to General Maximiliano Hernández Martínez as its hero.

Sharing Wealth and Power

The wealthy elite, who held the reins of economic power, usually cooperated with the military rulers. Known in the past as the Fourteen Families, they owned the land and business interests of the country. They served as cabinet ministers or advisers to the various governments and divided the spoils with them. Even now it is not unusual for senior officers to be taken into businesses. There were some individuals, both in the military and among the families, who saw the need for serious reforms in the country's social and economic structure, but they were unable to withstand the pressure of established interests. One incident illustrates the corruption within Salvadoran society: in 1976, the chief of staff of the Salvadoran army was arrested and jailed in the United States for attempting to sell some ten thousand submachine guns to American gangsters; he was released and returned home, but he was never charged.

In July 1979, Nicaraguan revolutionaries won a stunning victory over the strongman Anastasio Somoza, routing him completely. Several liberal Salvadoran army officers decided conditions must be changed in El Salvador before the same thing happened in their country. A new junta took power in October 1979, declaring a general amnesty for all political prisoners and those in exile. They also introduced the land reform program mentioned in Chapter 2.

An official investigation by the new junta disclosed enough evidence of wrongdoing to warrant the arrest of two former presidents. These actions inflamed the conservative military officers. They saw their positions threatened, closed ranks, and ousted the new junta. Those liberals and leftists who had hopes of working with the new government withdrew their support and joined already disaffected groups in the mountains. A civilian, José Napoleón Duarte, head of the Christian Democratic party, was given the presidency in 1980. He continued to press for land reform, but he was careful not to pull the reins too hard, and he left the military alone.

Conservative Salvadoran generals remained in power, resisting any change that might bring relief to the peasants and laborers in the country; every reform achieved was usually at the price of blood. The generals claimed they were holding the fortress against the onslaught of communism, when in actual fact they were strengthening the hand of the guerrillas by their toleration of, if not implication in, terror and murder. The following examples of their reign represent only the most noteworthy cases of injustice, those that made world headlines.

On March 24, 1980, Archbishop Oscar Arnulfo Romero was murdered while saying mass in a church in San Salvador. He had been very popular with the working people of El Salvador and had constantly spoken out against terrorist tactics and assassinations. The judge appointed to investigate the killing fled to Costa Rica when he learned too much. He claimed the assassination was planned by two army officers. One of them, according to the judge, was General José Alberto Medrano, founder of the death squad called ORDEN. ORDEN had been organized in the late 1960s and soon was alleged to have some 80,000 members—in effect, an independent army—with representatives in almost every village in El Salvador. While it was supposedly discontinued in 1979, after the liberal coup, some believed that it continued to operate. The second officer implicated in the archbishop's assassination was Roberto d'Aubuisson, an ex-major who denied any part in the murder.

In December 1980, four American missionary workers were murdered by members of the Salvadoran national guard. It took three and a half years to bring five guardsmen to trial and convict them of that crime. The impetus for the trial was a bill passed by the United States Congress in November 1983 that withheld 30 percent of military aid for

El Salvador until the five were tried. After an investigation for the State Department, an American judge implied that members of the Salvadoran government did everything possible to hide the powerful men who ordered the murders.

On January 3, 1981, two American and one Salvadoran land-reform specialists were gunned down by assassins while eating in a hotel in San Salvador. It took two years before two enlisted national guardsmen were indicted. They in turn implicated at least two army officers and two businessmen. The courts have cleared all four.

In 1982, Joan Didion, an American writer, was in El Salvador. She subsequently published a book about her experience, in which she succinctly describes the prevalence of death there:

The dead and pieces of the dead turn up in El Salvador everywhere, every day, as taken for granted as in a nightmare, or a horror movie. Vultures of course suggest the presence of a body. Bodies turn up in the brush of vacant lots, in the garbage thrown down ravines in the richer districts, in the public rest rooms, in bus stations.

These victims are some of the more than forty thousand people who have been killed in the civil war since 1979. This count usually includes only civilians killed, not guerrillas or uniformed members of the armed forces who have died in action. Both the guerrillas and the military are responsible for these deaths. The guerrillas, for instance, killed three conservative members of the Constituent Assembly in 1984; in May 1983, they assassinated an

American adviser in San Salvador. Both the military and the guerrillas have been guilty of killing peasants whom they suspected of collaborating with the other side. Thousands of these deaths have been attributed to death squads that have been allowed to operate freely.

A New Order

In 1982, under prodding by the United States government, which was supplying all the military and economic aid that kept the Salvadoran generals in power, elections were held in order to create a provisional government that would write a new constitution. The United States and liberal Salvadoran leaders believed that a fair election and a new civilian government could stem the guerrilla movement as well as military repression, bring peace to El Salvador, and open the way for economic and social reform. The guerrillas and their political representatives, however, boycotted the elections, claiming death squads would kill them if they campaigned openly for office.

A right-wing coalition headed by Roberto d'Aubuisson won, and its members were ready to take over the congressional and executive branches. A group of army officers however, refused to let d'Aubuisson take office for fear his nomination would mean the end of United States aid; the American ambassador to El Salvador sanctioned the move to keep d'Aubuisson out of the presidency. The generals chose Alvaro Alfredo Magaña, an inoffensive banker and member of an old ruling family in El Salvador.

While this election was a defeat for liberal forces, a new chance came in 1984, when a four-year president was slated to be elected under the new constitution. In May of that year José Napoleón Duarte defeated Roberto d'Aubuisson in a runoff election, much to the relief of United States officials and Salvadoran liberals. The guerrillas had refused to participate in this election as well.

In spite of threats to kill the United States ambassador and cries of fraudulent vote counting by d'Aubuisson, Duarte took office without incident. That moment was undoubtedly of great satisfaction to him. In 1972, he had been deprived of the presidency by the military, arrested, tortured, and then sent into exile for eight years. Like Alfonsin in Argentina, or Zuazo in Bolivia, he had powerful forces arrayed against him. The difference was that Duarte faced a strong, active guerrilla movement and a military that had not been cowed. While there was a strong desire for peace in El Salvador, opinions of how to achieve it varied widely. The question was, could Duarte bring all the forces together and become president of all El Salvador?

Conservative officers in the military did give way to the new government. Colonel Nicolás Carranza was relieved of his position as chief of the treasury police and sent abroad. The new chief promised to rein in the police and began by disbanding an intelligence unit that had been linked to death squad killings. Some army officers who had been implicated in assassinations were also transferred to foreign posts. Duarte hoped to defuse the guerrilla movement by opening negotiations with their political representatives. After two meetings in late 1984, hopes were high but results few. These negotiations will probably be long and frustrating, with each side maneuvering for the best possible terms. In the meantime, the civil war continues to make the people suffer. In this peace process, Duarte cannot afford to alienate the generals; he needs them to prevent the guerillas from taking over the country. At the same time, the new president faces the old problems of the need for land reform, high unemployment, labor and peasant unrest, and the conservative forces that will continue to resist change. Duarte has his work cut out for him.

Guatemala

If you are with us, we'll feed you, if not, we'll kill you.
—Guatemalan army officer

Since Guatemala secured its independence in 1823, it has been ruled primarily by military dictators and *caudillos*. In the twentieth century there have been short periods of political enlightenment when progress was made in social and economic reform, labor unions functioned, and the electoral process worked. But the constitutional reforms were always destroyed by new coups brought on by fear of change, expressed in this century as fears of "communist plots" by financial and business interests, conservative military leaders, and foreign residents with financial and political interests in the country. To most such groups, profits and position were more important than social justice.

In 1954, Carlos Castillo Armas, backed by the CIA, led a successful attack against the government of Jacobo Arbenz Guzman. Arbenz had pushed too hard for land reform and had brought communists into his government. After 1954, the new regimes gave in more and more to the old pressures of conservative interests. The opposition led an unsuccessful coup in the mid-1960s, after which its members fled to the mountains and formed guerrilla bands. They have not been strong enough to topple the government, however, and a low-key war has continued ever since.

In retaliation, the government has come down hard on its citizens and eliminated all civil and personal freedoms. There were no land reform programs to provide a more equitable distribution of rural holdings; unions went underground because of frequent persecutions; independent political leaders who represented a threat to the status quo were assassinated; military men continued to hold the presidency and dominate government. Abuses of human and civil rights became so flagrant under General Romeo Lucas Garcia that in 1977, when the United States government threatened to cut off all military aid to the country, the Guatemalan general got the jump on it and refused all assistance.

Paramilitary right-wing death squads often put together death lists. Anyone who voices objections to the means used for "pacifying" the people or who protests the presence of the military in an area gets added to the list. Kidnappings have also been fairly common. The fate of *desaparecidos* was a concern of Guatemalans even before the problem arose in Argentina and Chile.

Ríos Montt, an ex-general who took power and ruled in 1982–83, did bring some degree of calm to the countryside. Soldiers became less brutal and provided a helping and protective hand to the peasants. He also lifted some of the severe restrictions on political parties and the press, thereby creating much needed freedom of expression in the society. Soon, however, church officials and army officers began to criticize his policies. He returned to some of the earlier restrictions when an ousted junta member declared he was going underground to plot Ríos Montt's overthrow.

There were rumors of a coup for several months, so when it finally came it was not unexpected. On August 8, 1983, Ríos Montt's defense minister, Brigadier General Oscar Humberto Mejía Victores, became the new president. He is cut to the old pattern of the military in Latin America. One reporter said that his "virtues" are those of an army: he stresses national security, anti-communism, strong nationalism, and a liberal attitude toward business. He is, in other words, conservative, traditional, dedicated to the honor of the military, and not likely to tolerate too much reform.

A New Government

One of the reasons the junta turned Ríos Montt out of the presidency was that he seemed reluctant to give up his position and call an election for a Constituent Assembly to write a new constitution.

Mejía Victores said when he took power that he intended to "lead the Guatemalan people along democratic essentially nationalistic paths that will lead them to well-being in all its forms." He allowed elections to take place in July 1984. No leftists took part, but moderate to conservative parties ran 1,100 candidates for 88 seats. While moderates won the popular vote, Mejía Victores's government apportioned seats so that a rightist coalition had a fair chance to dominate the assembly. Observers claim that the military will give power to civilians only if they get a constitution and presidency that is conservative. In contrast to El Salvador, Guatemalan rulers evidently have no intention of losing their hold on the country. That they have moved toward any form of democratic government at all is probably due to their need for economic aid. By reducing human rights violations and allowing some political tolerance, the generals may get help from the United States in relieving Guatemala's 40 percent unemployment and its economy, which is almost at a standstill.

Religion and Revolution

4

Two Movements, Many Faces

As we have seen, the Catholic church has been part of Latin American society since the coming of the Spanish and Portuguese. Today Catholicism in Latin America has two faces: a traditional, conservative role supporting the established aspects of society on the one hand, and a new radical attitude encouraging change on the other.

Marxism is comparatively recent in the area. Marxism and socialism have existed in Latin America since the nineteenth century, soon after such ideas first took hold in Europe. After the Bolshevik Revolution in October 1917 in Russia, Marxism developed an aggressive ideology under the name of communism, intent on fomenting revolutions in other countries. Now also known as Marxism-Leninism, Soviet communism makes use of subversion and violent means to take power in countries and then hold them by organizing totalitarian governments.

Communist ideology calls for public ownership of all production and communication facilities and government responsibility for the welfare of individuals. Socialists also share this belief, but in contrast to communists, they do not resort to subversion and violence to achieve their goals. Many countries in the West today have governments that provide services that can be considered socialist in varying degrees, but those governments are not totalitarian or repressive.

By the 1920s the depressed groups in the population in Latin America were being tapped by the communists as a political and revolutionary force. The communists were not particularly successful, however, and their parties remained small and weak. Communism's appeal has been mainly to the urban worker, and the countries of Latin America are composed primarily of rural communities whose Indians and peasants have been tradition-ally wary of outsiders. Also, the urban movements, like Peronismo, took the ground out from under the communists.

The only successful Marxist nation in Latin America today is Cuba. It is a client state of the Soviet Union, heavily dependent on Soviet economic and military aid. In return, Cuba has sent its troops to fight on the side of Marxist forces in Angola, Ethiopia, and other places in behalf of the Soviet Union. The aggressive, anti-capitalist nature of the Cuban government is well established, and its rulers have backed guerrilla activities in other Latin American countries. It can be assumed that the Soviet Union has approved of these actions in the hope that new Marxist governments will be established in other Latin American countries.

Revolutionary movements in Latin America are usually genuinely national in character; they are reactions to repression and injustice, and they are carried out by various groups who seek change. It is only natural that such movements will attract the support of a country like Cuba at some point in their struggle. As a result, Marxists and liberationists within the Catholic church sometimes find themselves on the same side of the struggle in Latin America; other times they clash and become irreconcilable opponents. We need to examine and understand the roles of the church and Marxism before we can have a clear picture of the reform movements in Latin America today.

The Church in History

Since the arrival of the Spanish and Portuguese in Latin America, the Catholic church has maintained a strong presence in the region. In the beginning, the missionaries helped to alleviate the cruelty of the ruling conquistadores. They became the conscience of Spain, crying out against the harsh treatment and enslavement of the Indians and later, the blacks. The most famous of these missionaries was Bartolomé de Las Casas (1474–1566), a great humanitarian known today as the Apostle of the Indies.

After the church was established in the new world, it accumulated vast land holdings, built sumptuous cathedrals, and founded important universities, becoming one of the centers of power in Latin America. After the independence movement in the early nineteenth century, the church temporarily lost its secular power because it had favored continuation of Spanish rule. It rebounded, however, and was soon supporting the new ruling hierarchies. The church was well integrated into the power structures. Catholic dogma and ritual were considered part of the trappings of power, and church authorities often willingly reinforced a ruler's position. Until very recently many of the governments in Latin America maintained the old Spanish monarchical rights called *patronato real*, wherein they named the bishops and paid the salaries of the clergy.

At the same time, the church played a paternalistic role in the life of the common people—the peasants, laborers, and Indians. This meant performing acts of charity, primarily, providing the people with some of their material needs and emphasizing that one should look for rewards in the next world.

The Indians, peasants, *mestizos, ladinos, criollos*, mulattos, and *zambos*, remained religious under this system, but they adapted Catholicism to their own spiritual needs and beliefs. They saw God as no different from the political hierarchies they had lived with for so long. God represented power, but one could never be sure how he would use that power. They found more solace and hope in those who might intercede for them before God, especially the Virgin Mary, the mother of Jesus. It was she who became the ideal mother, like their own mothers, who cared for the family and held the home intact while the father faced the world, trying to keep his family alive. Christ, in contrast, was always pictured as suffering, as the free soul who had been captured and impaled on the cross. He was the image of the father faced with the uncertainty of life outside the home.

Certain native cult groups have operated in Latin America for centuries. Sometimes African gods and goddesses are honored along with Catholic saints in their ceremonies, and the same people may attend Catholic masses and also cult rites. The Indians have brought their old gods into the Catholic hierarchy of saints as well.

The church, by a kind of benign neglect, forced the common people to fall back on their families and immediate communities in order to find the spiritual support they needed. Their traditions and beliefs were passed down through generations and have lasted to the present day. These beliefs and superstitions reflect the life the people have lived in the real world, a hard life governed by landowners, police, political powers, and church officials, all of them seeming to be unalterable and distant yet omnipresent. This was the way the church was seen by its flock right up to the middle of this century.

The Church Today

Since the end of World War II, the Catholic church

in Latin America has undergone a series of changes that have both weakened and strengthened it. The focus of these changes can be said to be a conference in 1968, when the bishops of Latin America met to consider the role of the church in social and political life.

In spite of continued resistance on the part of conservatives within the church, the Medellín Conference specifically addressed social, political, and economic injustice in the countries of Latin America. What came forth was a call for revolution. The bishops rebuked the institutions and classes that exercised power; they also condemned foreign economic and political influence, especially that of the United States, which treated the Latin American countries like colonies. As Peggy Lernoux, a longtime resident of Latin America, put it, "Medellín produced the Magna Carta of today's persecuted, socially committed church, and as such rates as one of the major political events of the century: it shattered the centuries-old alliance of church, military, and rich elites."

Other forces were at work before the Medellín Conference, and in retrospect, we can see that they pointed the way toward this Magna Carta. One goes all the way back to the period immediately following World War II. At that time many foreign missionaries came to Latin America from the United States and Europe. As outsiders, they saw clearly that the traditional authoritarian rule of both the church and the elite contributed to the backwardness of the populace. They believed the church had to minister to the daily needs of the people, not simply be content with performing religious rites, and so they set off to live with their parishioners and share their misery. This social sense was caught up by some of the native priests of Latin America, as well. A further step was the Second Vatican Council, held in Rome from 1965 to 1969. That council stressed the importance of serving the people and the need to make the liturgy more meaningful to them. Both points reinforced the view of reformers in Latin America.

Another telling influence for change was the successful revolution carried out by Fidel Castro in Cuba in 1959. Even though the church in Cuba became less powerful after the social reform of the communists there, some Latin American priests turned to Cuban Marxism for answers to the problems confronting their regions. One was Camilo Torres, a Colombian priest trained in Louvain, Belgium. In Louvain, at the Catholic University, his studies in sociology led him ultimately to join the guerrillas in his native land. He was killed in 1966 and became a martyr in the eyes of the leftists of Latin America.

Torres became the symbol of an enlightened church linked to the Marxist revolutionary philosophy. Those who believed in this union were convinced it could transform Latin American society by creating new spiritual and civil standards under a government of social and economic justice.

The church authorities were not convinced and resisted the new radical movement as they had the moderate movement for reform. Priests and nuns, however, continued to desert the hierarchy and join the quest for social justice through other means that appealed to them. By the time of the Medellín Conference there was ample reason for the Latin American bishops to join the new crusade, not only to seek justice for people, but to save the church as well.

The Protestant Witness

The work of Protestant missionaries in Latin America, who are usually referred to as evangelicals, provided another impetus for reform in the Catholic church. Although few in number, they have never been held back by an old, established hierarchy. They had no place to go but straight to the peasant and Indian communities where they worked closely with the people. Usually, their goals were nonpolitical and practical as well as religious.

These evangelicals believe it is vital to make families realize that they can take some immediate measures to reduce their own misery. If, for instance, they can get a father to stop wasting his time and money on alcohol, they can help him lead a more productive life. They teach the people to improve their diet by eating eggs instead of selling them for a few coins. The evangelicals also show the people how to fight disease by keeping themselves and their homes clean. Such changes do not represent final solutions, only some elementary means of coping with the environment. It is a start. Yet the achievement of even these small improvements requires patience, tact, and constant presence on the part of the missionaries.

Catholic missionaries also introduced such programs and goals, which were known as grass-roots communities, in which the priest lives and works alongside his parishioners. Their efforts also included land reform—a movement, as we have seen, that elicits violent reactions on the part of large landowners and their backers in government. It is very difficult to avoid becoming enmeshed in politics when establishing such communities.

Liberating Theology

In 1971, Gustavo Gutiérrez, a Peruvian priest, who, like Torres, had studied at Louvain, published a book on the theology of liberation. His view was unique and helped provide the practical underpinning for a rejuvenated Catholic church in Latin America. Gutiérrez distinguished between *salvation*—the work of the individual in relation with God—and *liberation*—the work of the individual in relation with fellow human beings. By liberating the depressed peasant from exploitation, for instance, one does not ensure the peasants' salvation in the eyes of God; that is up to the peasants themselves. But liberation does help the person who attempts it, for it is a Christian act that is good in the eyes of God. In addition, this theology states that peasants are more likely to work out their own salvation in a just society than under an authoritarian regime whose repression will lead them to despair, estranged from God and captives to superstitions and cult rituals.

Gutiérrez relied on Marxism for his interpretation of society's ills, but he rejected its ultimate, totalitarian solution. Although he and his followers believe that a socialist government is the best solution to the problems of Latin America, they do not think that a communist government, with its authoritarian character, leads to a Christian community of peace and justice. In other words, they see the negative side of Fidel Castro's system in Cuba and want no part of such a government. Gutiérrez also hopes to awaken the poor to their condition as a prelude to taking their destinies in their own hands.

One Church, Many Churches

Such ideas opened up the church and split it into many factions, some of which joined with Marxists, socialists, or members of other Christian sects and became activists according to their own beliefs. Conservatives within the church still fought against change; they wanted to continue the work they had done in the past. They believed their role was to look after the well-being of souls, not to administer to social ills.

Those religious leaders on the front lines of the Latin American struggle for a new life are committed to live with their parishioners, working side by side with them in their everyday world, urging on them the need to organize themselves to secure the social and economic necessities of life. They have become representatives of what they call the "horizontal church," a church that exists on the same level with the people, sharing life and death with them.

Statistics give some indication of the work of these activists. In 1968 only 21 percent of the priests and nuns in Latin America were working with the poor; in 1978 the figure was 40 percent. They were generally the younger clergy, under age forty-four, well educated and even trained in practical courses to help them cope with their environment. Thus, their vows of poverty became more than just a token for these people; they represented a real commitment to the betterment of the conditions around them.

But statistics tell another story as well. Dangers come with this commitment. Since the Medellín Conference in 1968, close to a thousand priests, nuns, and bishops have been arrested, tortured, or have been murdered. Others have been expelled from the country in which they worked. Thousands of the lay people who joined them to found grass-roots communities have also been imprisoned or murdered. Three Maryknoll nuns and one lay missionary, for example, were murdered in El Salvador in 1980. They are among the many who have paid for their dedication to a better life for all the people of Latin America.

God Has No Ideology

Part of the Catholic church in Latin America may be committed to social revolution, but to most Marxist guerrillas that is of no significance. What the church offers in its revolution, they say, is nonviolent resistance to rulers who have no conscience. Pacificism will not lead to power, and if by some miracle followers of the church should obtain power, they have no political program to keep them there. The people need leadership as well as compassion.

All religious groups are welcome to crusade for liberty as far as the Marxist guerrillas are concerned, but they should be under no illusions as to the ultimate objective—political power. *Patria o muerte* (fatherland or death) is not an empty phrase for them. While it is true that the religious activists have died and are dying for essentially the same cause as the guerrillas, most of them will never bear arms against the enemy. For the Marxists, *muerte* means kill or be killed; for the Christians, it means only the possibility of being killed for doing God's work.

Of course there are many shades of opinion between these two extreme points of view. Many people are more or less on one side or the other. It is no accident that among the heroes of Latin Americans are people as diverse as Martin Luther King, Jr., a black American pacifist of the Gandhian tradition, and Ernesto "Che" Guevara, a Marxist revolutionary; it is also no accident that a theologian like Gustavo Gutiérrez drew his inspiration from Marxist principles.

The theories of Karl Marx on the exploitation of the working class, on capitalism, imperialism, and the proper path to revolution have thus found adherents in Latin America among leftist clergy, university students, union members, middle-class people, and liberals of many persuasions, as well as being the basic belief of the orthodox communist parties.

The Cuban Revolution

Many Latin American leftists first saw the possibility of seizing power after the Cuban revolution of 1959, probably the most cataclysmic recent political event in Latin America. The Cuban revolution provided a geographical and political base in Latin America for a sharp struggle against those same elites which the church of liberation opposes.

Castro and his guerrilla army took power from the Batista regime in Cuba, a typical Latin Amerian repressive government. Soon after, Castro and his followers declared themselves to be communists. They nationalized all the island's industries and businesses; created a land reform program, which included confiscating land from private owners; and refused to pay indemnity to them or to the American firms that had investments in the country. These steps naturally created hostile reactions in the United States. A ban has been placed on the import of Cuban products ever since, chiefly sugar and cigars, and American firms are not allowed to trade there. Cuba turned to the Soviet Union for its economic survival and has since been a client state of that country.

The Soviets regard Cuba as a political victory in the East-West confrontation. But economically it is a disaster to the cost of some $4 billion a year, the price of Soviet Union must pay to keep this communist state alive in Latin America. This price included buying Cuban sugar at inflated prices to give the impression that it is trade and not aid that is given, and supplying material and guidance to almost every aspect of the growing Cuban economy and military might.

In the 1960s, Castro supported revolutionary movements in Bolivia, Colombia, Peru, Venezuela, and Guatemala. He was sure that if revolution worked for him it would work for other Latin American countries. Nowhere was he successful. He simply provoked powerful anti-communist and anti-Castro reactions in these countries. In many instances, he even went against the judgments of the established communist parties there, putting the Soviet Union in the difficult position of having to pacify both Castro and local communists, trying to keep the loyalty of both.

At home, Castro keeps tight political control on the Cuban people. He has been elected president for life and his brand of communism runs the country. He is much in the historical mold of the old *caudillo*, with some modern differences, including the Marxist emphasis on improved physical well-being of the citizen, and a cultural life that remains active and free as long as it does not attack any of the tenets laid down by the ruling regime. In general, Cubans are healthier, more literate, and better housed and fed than the poor and near-poor in other Latin American countries. This is not to say that conditions are reaching a luxurious level there, but the grinding poverty of other countries in the region is absent.

Marjorie Moore is an American who has lived in Cuba since 1950. She arrived as an upper-class citizen and now lives in a small area of a once spacious apartment, sharing the remainder with her two daughters and their husbands. While she told an Associated Press reporter she didn't like communism—meaning, we must assume, the lack of personal freedom—she was in favor of Castro's revolution and believes it has given self-esteem to the Cubans. The Associated Press reported her as saying that the Cuban communists have wiped out the "worst poverty, ignorance and illness, the things that distressed her in her younger days."

Others do not have such a fine opinion of Cuba. Since Castro took power in 1959, several hundred thousand Cubans have fled their homeland. These include people from the lower to the upper classes, people disenchanted with Castro's idea of democracy and unwilling to give up their freedom to a collective ideal. Some of those not lucky enough to get out landed in prison, accused of counterrevolutionary activity, espionage, or refusal to adapt to the communist society. Life in prison is reported to be harsh for political prisoners, with little attention given to their most basic needs, such as proper diet and sanitary facilities. Some of these prisoners are not released after they have served their terms. The Cuban-American National Foundation in Washington, D.C., estimates that there are from five thousand to ten thousand political prisoners in Cuban penal institutions.

Nonetheless, Fidel Castro became a hero among various leftist groups in Latin America. His early followers, both in Cuba and outside, called themselves Fidelistas. Even those liberals and leftists who did not agree with his tactics admired his revolution. He had achieved what no other country in Latin America had done; he tweaked the nose of Uncle Sam and remained alive to boast of it. In 1961, at the Bay of Pigs Castro defeated a United States–supported attempt by Cuban exiles to invade the country and overthrow the communists. In doing this, Castro inspired both hope and fear in Latin America. The military leaders, on the one hand, saw his system as a threat to their existence and as proof of communist aggression; the guerrilla movements, on the other hand, saw Cuba as a much-needed base of support for revolutionary activities in their own countries.

Fidelismo became more and more evident as the 1980s progressed; Cuba was still the inspiration for successful and potential revolutions in Latin America. Fidel remained buoyantly aggressive and truculent, but after twenty-five years of power at home and failures in other Latin American countries, he must now realize that he will not remake the Latin American world in quick fashion. Certain events, however, have given him reason for encouragement; his destiny is not yet played out. By mid-1984, a new hope lay in the five-year-old Sandinista government in Nicaragua and the successes of the guerrillas in El Salvador. Partisans on all sides hotly debated whether these movements could create new Cuban-style independent states.

Nicaragua in Revolution

One September day in 1980, the headline in *Barricada* (Barricade), the official newspaper of the Sandinistas in Nicaragua, read as follows, "He Died like a Dog on a Corner." It referred to the assassination of Anastasio Somoza Debayle in Asunción, Paraguay, where he had gone to live after he was driven from his dictatorship in Nicaragua in 1979. Somoza and a business associate were riding in a white Mercedes-Benz, which was blown to bits not far from his mansion. The assassins were never found, although the police in Asunción claimed they killed one of the leaders in a gun battle. There has never been any connection established between this deed and the Sandinista government, much as they celebrated it.

In Nicaragua, there was great elation over Somoza's death. People drank to his demise in the bars and read the *Barricada* headline with satisfaction. His country hated him. The Somoza family had run Nicaragua as its personal fiefdom ever since Anastasio Somoza García, the father, took power through a coup in 1936. This older Somoza had been chief of the national guard and as president continued to keep it under his control, using it whenever necessary to keep order. The father was assassinated in 1956, after which the only brother of young Anastasio, Luis Somoza Debayle, became president. His rule was somewhat milder. There were a few figurehead presidents as well, but the Somoza family was always in control. Young Anastasio had graduated from West Point, and when he took command of the country in 1967, he brought all the tactics of a harsh miltiary regime to bear on the people.

Over the period of Somozan rule, the country's economic resources went through a cycle of development and decline. The regime favored large landholders and a growing middle class, both of which depended on an export and import market. The lower classes did not participate in any change for the better. Instead they became more and more impoverished because their wages and conditions always remained depressed. City and rural slums grew despite the economic expansion. By the 1970s, when the world economy began to slow down, Nicaragua, like other Latin American countries, also suffered economic setbacks. Funds became scarce, and even those groups that had cooperated with the Somozas began to grumble. In addition, corruption was exposed in the highest levels of government, including the Somoza family. It has been said that by the late 1970s Somoza and his cronies owned 50 percent of all the arable land and 40 percent of all industry. In short, all the destructive elements of authoritarian rule flourished in Nicaragua.

As early as 1961 the Sandinista Front for National Liberation (FSLN in Spanish) was formed to fight against the Nicaraguan regime. Carlos Fonseca Amador and Tomás Borge were two of the founders. Fonseca was later killed in a battle with the National Guard; Borge survived and is interior minister in the Sandinista government today. The FSLN took the name Sandinista in honor of Augusto César Sandino, a Nicaraguan who fought a guerrilla war against United States intervention in Nicaraguan political and economic life, a war that lasted from 1927 to 1933. After peace was declared, Sandino was invited to dinner at the presidential palace. In spite of assurances of safe conduct, Sandino was assassinated after the dinner by Anastasio Somoza's national guard.

From time to time the FSLN changed its tactics, but it never wavered on two principles: it refused ever to cooperate with the Somoza government, and it always maintained its Marxist ideology. By the middle 1970s, the Sandinistas had acquired considerable experience in both urban and rural guerrilla warfare and were ready to broaden their attacks on the Somoza government. They came more and more to believe that the majority of Nicaraguans would rally around their cause. The non-Marxist opposition had also become disenchanted with Somoza and finally did join the FSLN in a broad political and military front after Pedro Chamorro, a well-known and popular liberal, was murdered.

Pedro Joaquín Chamorro had been editor of *La Prensa*, an independent newspaper in Managua. As such he was a constant moral thorn in the side of the corrupt Somoza regime. On January 10, 1978, while driving to work, he was cornered by two cars and shot down. Doctors counted thirty gunshot wounds in his body. Though Somoza could not be directly linked to the killing, members of his family and government were. From that point until July 1979, Somoza and his National Guard fought a losing battle against the outrage of the Nicaraguans, led by the military leadership of the FSLN.

By the time Somoza was finally defeated, Nicaragua was a shambles: 40,000 people dead; 100,000 wounded; 40,000 children orphaned; 200,000 families homeless. The people faced a year without an agricultural harvest, cities were bombed out, one-third of the labor force was out of work, and health care, never developed by Somoza in the first place, was in worse condition than ever. Industry was in a similar sad state. There was a $1.5 billion foreign debt that had to be paid if Nicaragua hoped to keep its credit and obtain more loans.

Right from the beginning, the Sandinistas meant to save the Marxist revolution. They created a Government of National Reconstruction and formed a ruling junta, which initially included representatives from the non-Marxist groups that had participated in the revolution.

One of their first moves was to form local citizens' committees, even down to city blocks, to help reorganize society. Based on the Cuban model, they were first called Civil Defense Committees; then they were renamed Sandinista Defense Committees (CDS in Spanish). The local CDS elected representatives to sit on zonal councils; the zonal councils were represented in larger neighborhood councils; and finally the larger councils elected representatives to sit on a city council. All these councils, called Peoples' Committees, were called on to supervise and coordinate reconstruction in four areas: food, health and hygiene, medicine, and distribution of information. A fifth concern covered vigilance and defense until a police force and an army could be formed.

At the same time, the new junta set about creating agricultural cooperatives on the land that had belonged to Somoza. It also nationalized the industries he owned—some 155 companies—and formed a trade union. Banks were nationalized; no foreign credit could be negotiated or money sent abroad without government approval. Anyone who was a declared Somocista could keep no property or assets. The junta did say, however, that it expected private enterprise to continue ownership of 75 percent of industry, and to generate 60 percent of the gross national product in the years ahead.

Almost immediately, controversy broke out in the new Nicaragua. The Sandinistas were determined to keep control of the revolution, but the non-Marxist middle class expected a more open society. Opponents accused the government of delaying a date for nationwide elections. Although it allowed private businesses to function, business leaders claimed the junta so hemmed them in with regulations that they could not prosper. As a result, both the economy and the population were suffering.

La Prensa, which had been taken over by one of Chamorro's sons, remained independent and continually criticized the ruling junta.

As a result, the junta subjected it to censorship and usually cut out the paper's criticisms, only adding fuel to the opposition's charges.

Opponents also claimed that the military and police were not to be trusted because they had been formed from Sandinista guerrilla units. The local defense committees, which were kept after the country began to recover from the initial destruction, were accused of being nothing more than networks of spies for the junta.

Private business suffered, funds were short; prices, exports, and imports were carefully controlled by the junta. Many members of the middle class gave up trying and left the country. Others stayed to fight for their rights on the scene. One of these was Enrique Bolanos Geyer, in 1984 head of the Superior Council of Private Enterprise in Managua. He never supported the Sandinista movement and wanted to move it away from Marxist goals toward a more traditional democratic system.

The Catholic church establishment also remained a center of conflict with the government. Archbishop Miguel Obando y Bravo had led his flock, often in opposition to the government, through the Somoza years and then began treading a similar path of opposition against the Sandinistas. He accused them of being only a political party, not a government. In essence, he rejected their claim that the revolution of 1979 was theirs alone.

At the end of 1983, Bishop Pablo Antonio Vega Mantilla was elected head of the Nicaraguan Episcopal Conference, the guiding body of the Roman Catholic church in Nicaragua. Bishop Vega spoke in the spirit of the new church but was careful to keep his political distance from any government. He saw the church in Latin America as possessed of a radical spirit that could bring on human liberation, but not political freedom. He criticized the Sandinista junta because it lacked "Christian values."

A popular church did arise in Nicaragua which opposed the established institution of bishops Obando and Vega. Composed of priests and people who support the Sandinista government, it carried on duties independent of Archbishop Obando's wishes. Naturally the popular church was condemned by the bishops. Vega declared that it was not really a church since it did not lead to God but had joined forces with powerful political leaders instead of working for the good of people. The split in the Catholic church in Nicaragua was thus a reflection not only of the split in the Latin American church, but within the liberal wing of the church as well. The two most prominent figures in the popular church are Ernesto Cardenal, a priest who serves in the junta and is minister of culture; and Miguel d'Escoto Brockman, a Maryknoll priest who is foreign minister. Pope John Paul II has told these priests to give up their political activity, but they have refused.

The New Nicaragua

Regardless of these conflicts, Nicaragua was still a safer place to be in than El Salvador or Guatemala in 1984. There were no death squads roaming the streets. To those who fought alongside the FSLN in 1979, however, that safety is not enough. They believe that whatever security and freedom there is will be short-lived, and they fear that the junta will impose tighter communist control on the country as it gains more power. The opponents say this will deprive them of the right to a free, democratic Nicaragua, something they fought and risked their lives for. Nicaragua will then become a new Cuba, they say, only this time on the mainland of Central America. From this stronghold, Cuba, backed by the Soviet Union, will move on to other countries, most especially El Salvador. Gradually all the other countries of Central America will fall into their orbit. This projection is called the domino theory: the idea that under the communist conspiracy directed by the Soviet Union, when one nation goes communist all the surrounding nations will follow.

The Sandinistas deny that this will happen. They claim their interest is in the success of their Nicaraguan revolution. Daniel Ortega Saavedra, the coordinator of the junta, has said that the Sandinistas' roots are "profoundly Nicaraguan." While he and his fellow Marxists do not deny their allegiance to Marxist theories, they always insist on being called Sandinistas, to emphasize their own style and beliefs. Cuba was and remains a major source of moral and material aid in their struggle. There are reported to be up to six thousand Cubans in Nicaragua acting in various capacities from teachers to military advisers. But the Sandinistas maintain they are beholden to no other nation and will answer to no other nation.

Whether the Sandinistas should be considered a threat to the security of Central and Latin America depends on one's view concerning the strength of the communist conspiracy and the ability of the Soviet Union to force nations outside its immediate sphere to do its bidding.

The administration of President Ronald Reagan in the United States has seen the threat as very real. His government has backed the Nicaraguan Democratic Force, an anti-Sandinista group based in Honduras and composed of about ten thousand fighters. Because there are ex–national guard members in the force, the Sandinistas refer to them as Somocistas. Opponents of the Sandinistas call them "Contras," meaning counterrevolutionaries. The Sandinistas introduced a Law of Emergency, giving the junta the right to move against perceived internal enemies and to keep the country in a state of readiness to fight against the Contras. Some people have been arrested as a result, and there are claims of bad treatment. There has been no proof of torture or the type of abuse received at the hands of the Somoza minions, however. The Contras slowed development in certain areas of the economy and generally harassed the area near the Honduran border, where people have been killed.

Another anti-Sandinista movement is the Nicaraguan Democratic Revolutionary Alliance, headed by Eden Pastora Gómez, a former Sandinista and member of the junta. He broke with them in 1981, accusing the Sandinistas of having betrayed the revolution, of having sold out to the communists.

The Alliance began its life in Costa Rica and then was asked to leave by that government. It then created a base in the southeast jungles of Nicaragua. At this point neither the Contras nor the Alliance has aroused the Nicaraguans to rebellion.

Election

In March 1984, the Sandinistas issued a law that set the rules for an election to be held on November 4, 1984. Voters were to elect a president, a vice-president, and a ninety-member legislature for six-year terms. The junta said the election would be open to all parties and individuals except those who had been connected with the Somozan regime and those who had joined anti-Sandinista guerrilla groups. The Sandinistas nominated Daniel Ortega Saavedra, coordinator of the junta, as their presidential candidate.

Major opposition parties, labor federations, and business groups objected to the terms of the election process. They wanted the Law of Emergency, which they believed would be used against them during the campaign, lifted. They also wanted press censorship stopped, political prisoners released, and all exiles allowed to return to Nicaragua. They demanded that the Sandinista Front remove itself from the government and give up its political control over the army, the police, and the national television network. Some also asked that the elections be held in January 1985, to give them more time to prepare for a campaign.

Shacks in Guayaquil, Ecuador.
Carlos Conde, Inter-American Development Bank

Indian laborers planting seedling eucalyptus trees on a hilly farm in Ecuador.

David Mangurian, Inter-American Development Bank

A street in the central market district of San Salvador, the capital of El Salvador.

David Mangurian, Inter-American Development Bank

The village school in Santa Ines, El Salvador.
Inter-American Development Bank

Running water has recently been brought to the rural village of Llano Largo, Panama.
David Mangurian, Inter-American Development Bank

A Guatemalan family standing in front of their new concrete block home, built under a government financed program.
David Mangurian, Inter-American Development Bank

A group of Nicaraguan farmers receiving a government loan to finance planting corn and beans.

David Mangurian, Inter-American Development Bank

War damage in Estili, Nicaragua.
Inter-American Development Bank

The Sandinistas had announced a twelve-week period for campaigning, running from August 3 to October 31. All opposition parties would have to share fifteen minutes a day on television and thirty minutes a day on radio as part of their campaign. On election day six parties ran candidates. The Sandinista candidate for president won 67 percent of the vote. Thus, the lines remain drawn. The Sandinistas claim they won a great victory; the opposition says the vote was incomplete. The future does not promise any relaxation of tension.

El Salvador
Venceremos (We Will Triumph)

Since 1981, the Reagan administration has claimed that the Sandinistas have acted as a conduit for arms shipment to the guerrillas in El Salvador. The Sandinistas have made no secret of their moral support of the guerrilla movement there and had even allowed its leaders to set up headquarters in Managua until October 1983. But they deny providing arms to the guerrillas. The Salvadoran guerrillas also have denied it, saying that, on the contrary, it took them over ten years to acquire and develop all the resources they now possess in order to carry on their struggle against the military government in El Salvador. They captured arms—including American M-16 rifles used in the Vietnam War—from the Salvadoran soldiers or bought them on the international arms market. Their support, they say, has come not from governments but from people and foreign organizations who back them or sympathize with their cause.

It would be naive, however, to assume that the Soviet Union and Cuba have not provided some kind of aid to the Salvadoran guerrillas. Medical supplies, equipment, and ammunitions for heavy weapons do get in. Some material has come by boat across the Gulf of Fonseca, some by land across southwest Honduras, which lies between Nicaragua and El Salvador. In 1983, the United States government reported that most material coming through Nicaragua was brought in at night by light planes. Flying low, under radar, the planes could land on deserted highways, unload quickly, and fly out again. The Salvadoran army reportedly has only limited ability to attack such night flights, because of poor communciations and slow response.

The guerrillas in El Salvador claim they can operate without such shipments from Nicaragua and have been doing so; they have said the area is now so heavily monitored that it would be difficult to bring anything in. In addition, both Cuba and Nicaragua proceed with caution in this area. Leaders in both countries believe the United States is planning an invasion of Nicaragua in order to overthrow the Sandinistas. They do not want to provide any excuse that may strengthen such a plan. Further, the Sandinistas rightly claimed that the United States government has produced no proof of arms shipment to the Salvador guerrillas. The Reagan government replied that to do so would compromise the intelligence sources that provide the information.

A former Salvadoran guerrilla commander, Arquímedes Canadas, has said that Cubans have directed the strategic operations of the Salvadoran guerrillas since 1980. If this is true, they have been careful to stay out of El Salvador and direct the operations from Havana or Managua. And they have been just as discreet where supply of weapons is concerned. The fighting is done by Salvadoran guerrillas.

In July 1983, the Sandinista regime said it accepted the principle of ending arms shipments across borders, an implication that Nicaragua as well as the United States has been supplying arms to combatants.

Civil War in El Salvador

In El Salvador the guerrilla movement is unified under the Farabundo Martí Front of National Liberation (FMLN in Spanish), which was created in 1980, and named for Augustin Farabundo Martí, one of the communists who was executed during La Matanza in 1932. There are five separate groups in FMLN, and they refer to themselves as political-military organizations.

One such organization, the People's Revolutionary Army (ERP) was founded in 1971 and is the largest of the guerrilla groups. Commanded by Jorge Meléndez and Joaquín Villalobos, it has had the most military success; its troops are considered well trained and disciplined. They also run the major clandestine broadcast station, Radio Venceremos, which reports on battles and political maneuvering in El Salvador and abroad.

The second largest guerrilla group is the Popular Liberation Forces (FPL), formed in 1970. Until April 1983 it was headed by Salvador Cayetano Carpio, a sixty-three-year-old radical communist who was not prone to join alliances.

The other three are the National Resistance (RN), formed in 1975 as a faction that left ERP, with strong connections among urban workers; the Central American Revolutionary Workers Party (PRTC), a small group founded in 1979; and the Communist Party of El Salvador (PCS), which dates back to 1931 and has a small military force.

Under the FMLN, these organizations have also formed a Unified Revolutionary Directorate (DRU) in order to coordinate their activities in the field. One can also see here the diversity that both Latin American politics and Marxism spawn.

The FMLN has had its ups and downs since 1980. Generally, it is strongest in the eastern provinces of Chalatenango and Morazán, but it has made forays into other areas as well, such as San Vicente and Usulután provinces. FMLN claims to control one-third of the country. In the summer of 1983, the Salvadoran government thought it had the guerrillas on the run, but by the end of the year several attacks had been made against the army that showed the guerrillas were still strong.

In spite of training by fifty American advisers stationed in El Salvador, the army does not have a reputation for military effectiveness. There have even been reports in American newspapers that the guerrillas bought ammunition from Salvadoran Army officers through middlemen. Under such leadership, soldiers lose their will to fight.

The FMLN has executed some of the soldiers it has taken prisoner, but they generally release them after capture. They believe this is more effective propaganda, for the soldiers will be less likely to fight after being freed. Some have even joined the rebels. As one guerrilla put it, "When we ask them what they are fighting for, they can only reply, 'a paycheck.' But we are fighting for *Patria*. That makes them think."

A Moment Lost

The FMLN has been well led, no matter who has been directing them. By mid-1984, they had arms and ten thousand to twelve thousand troops, up from about five thousand in 1980. They were determined and intended to make no important concessions to the corrupt system that ruled El Salvador. However, their strength was limited. They were not able to hold a position long once they had taken it, because they had to fade back into their own territory and regroup for further attacks. This is true of most guerrilla movements; they control a specific area but have difficulty expanding it.

The FMLN admitted that the population was not ready for a mass uprising. They had tried that in January 1981, and it had failed. This is their chief problem: El Salvador is not like Nicaragua or Cuba.

Canadas believes that such a revolutionary feeling existed in 1980, after the assassination of Archbishop Romero. There was a nationwide reaction, equivalent to the reaction to the murder of Chomorro in Managua in 1978. If the guerrillas had given the signal then, Canadas believes an insurrection would have taken place. The moment passed, however, and the guerrillas had to wait for a new opportunity.

Up to the spring of 1983, the guerrillas were not completely united either. Cayetano Carpio of the FPL, known in the field as Marcial, had been a strong leader, but he was very independent. When the FPL leaders voted to put the number two person in his place, Melida Anaya Montes, known as Ana Maria, Carpio had her assassinated in Managua. When his role in the crime was discovered, he committed suicide. The FPL discredited him and now fully recognizes the authority of the FMLN and DRU. This new situation probably accounts for the better coordination and new tactical success of the guerrillas. They became more than ever united in their attacks.

The election of José Napoleón Duarte as president of El Salvador in May 1984, helped to change the political climate there, giving a legitimacy to the government that had not existed before. This is true even though the left did not participate in the election. Duarte has expressed the hope that his administration can introduce much needed reforms and bring Salvadorans together to work peaceably for the good of their country. If he succeeds, the result could seriously undercut the guerrilla movement. If the army should become frightened and remove Duarte from office, the guerrillas may be presented with the long-awaited opportunity for a real revolution.

The Real Enemy

Although the unity of the guerrillas has made them more effective in the field and in peace negotiations, there may be less concord if they achieve a position of power similar to that of the Sandinistas. Within the FMLN there are Marxists, Marxist-Leninists who are guided by the Cuban and Soviet systems, and those sympathetic to Marxist principles but not necessarily to the methods of rule. Some, like Canadas, want a strictly national revolution; others realize that they must depend on the goodwill and support of the Cuban-Soviet bloc in order to survive, even if they don't accept all of the bloc's philosophy. In any leftist government in El Salvador there would undoubtedly be arguments and disappointments. Whether disagreements would create splits and new battles is an open question. Most likely they would, for men and women who fought for their beliefs and saw their comrades die for them would not give them up easily.

Today the FMLN is convinced it will eventually win. Certainly at this point its leaders have no intention of bargaining away their strength in any peace negotiations; they are in complete agreement on that. And like Nicaragua and Cuba, they also are in agreement that the real enemy is not any military regime that heads a government in Central America; their enemy is the United States, which is supporting the military regime. If the FMLN loses, it will be to the United States. Therefore, it is this eagle hovering above Latin America, guarding the bastions of traditional governments that, they all agree, has to be defeated. Other Latin Americans may not be so extreme in their judgment, but many of them, too, accept this judgment.

The
Eagle
Overhead

Carlos Rangel, a Venezuelan educated in the United States, has written about the relations between Latin America and the United States. In too many instances, he believes, the United States is the convenient whipping boy for all problems in the Southern Hemisphere.

No Latin American who pins the blame for his country's ills on North American imperialism need fear rebuttal. There is an almost general belief in Latin America today that the United States has siphoned off the wealth that could have led to the Southern Hemisphere's development. *They* are rich because *we* are poor; *we* are poor because *they* are rich. The argument is that, but for North American development, there would have been no Latin-American underdevelopment; that but for Latin American underdevelopment, there would have been no North American development.

Rangel goes on to say that the United States has also had a positive effect on Latin America but that this has been lost in the frustrations of Latin Americans trying to build free, independent nations. Latin Americans even forget, he says, that before World War I, the British and French were the predominant economic forces in the area, shaping regional policies to their advantage. Latin America's struggle took place against a different background than that of the United States. Efforts in Latin America to achieve independence were more turbulent, and traditions held the area in a tighter political and economic mold. Though the constitution and political system of the United States were admired and imitated, they were difficult to maintain in countries where *personalismo* (another term for the idea of the *caudillo*) and the gun were always supplanting governments. Most *caudillos* cooperated with foreigners, as long they received a share of the profits and their political power was not attacked. Other leaders saw this system of foreign dependency as the only way to develop their backward industries and natural resources, and they went along with it, though reluctantly. Any Latin American leader who tried to take away foreign control of an economy met with difficulties when the time came to borrow money abroad or to export the country's goods. And Latin America never organized into one or two large political units. The Southern Hemisphere remained divided and weak, a prey to outsiders including neighboring countries.

The United States simply took over the role of colonial leader already established by European financial and business centers. However, for about one hundred years before this hapened, the United States had maintained a strong political presence in Latin America. In the nineteenth century the United States began a series of military interventions, especially in Central America, that are now remembered with bitterness and mistrust. Some of these interventions supported American and European business interests in Latin America, and in this way foreign economic and political goals merged in the minds of many Latin Americans. Even more damaging was the fact that the United States government supported harsh military dictatorships that seemed to be acting only for United States interests.

In the twentieth century, and most especially after World War II, there has been a growth of nationalistic feeling in Latin America. Some leaders have sought to control their economies by decreasing or denying ownership to foreign companies. United States interests have too often resisted these efforts. In the 1930s, for instance, Mexico expropriated United States and British oil holdings in the country. The companies were paid off, but they enforced a world boycott against Mexican oil for thirty years. Such actions gave political groups on the left good reason to propose solutions to Latin American problems that excluded all intervention by foreign capitalists and their governments. Marxists and socialists have claimed that the United States is not just a meddling foreign power that must be curbed, but an imperial center that must be defeated.

Carlos Fuentes, a Mexican writer who has lived a long time in the United States, has pointed out that this attitude has come to be held not only by the political left but also by a much broader spectrum of people in Latin America.

The perception of the United States by Latin Americans as the paramount regional power in terms comparable to the perception of the Soviet Union by the people of Eastern Europe should not be underestimated. Many defects and errors of a revolutionary regime are pardoned or overlooked by the majority of its people because they feel that the new government has finally lifted the weight of American hegemony. . . . It follows that a revolutionary regime, on the basis of its anti-American posture, can mobilize the people for its radical goals.

A brief review of the Untied States political, military, and economic presence in Latin America will make this attitude more understandable.

Europe Keep Out

In 1823 President James Monroe issued the Monroe Doctrine which, in essence, said that the United States would stay out of European affairs and Europe should keep out of the Western Hemisphere. The doctrine did not speak against any colonies then held in the New World by the European powers, but it warned against creating any new ones. It was the first protective act by the United

States over the new countries in Latin America. The significance of the Monroe Doctrine is that it set forth a policy that United States governments have adhered to and enlarged upon ever since—that the Western Hemisphere is under its influence.

In 1833, the United States incurred the resentment of Argentina by backing British occupation of the Falkland Islands. The United States claimed they were legally a British colony received from Spain by treaty.

In 1848, the United States signed a treaty with Mexico that brought Texas, New Mexico, and California under American jurisdiction. Mexico was bullied into accepting the treaty and came close to being included in the deal as well. This action was partly the result of a theory known as Manifest Destiny, the belief that the United States was destined eventually to extend all the way across North America, from the Atlantic Ocean to the Pacific.

Before the Civil War, American citizens were mainly concerned with finding a passage across Central America that would cut down travel time between the East and West coasts of the United States. Panama (then part of Colombia), Nicaragua, and Mexico all possessed possible sites. By the time of the California gold rush in 1849, there were rough passages by canoe and mule across Panama and by steamboat through rivers and a lake in Nicaragua. In 1855, a railroad was completed across Panama. In spite of disease, bad climate, insects, and thieves, these enterprises made millions for their owners before they ceased operations.

There was also much political maneuvering at the time. In 1856, an American adventurer and misguided visionary named William Walker was legitimately elected president of Nicaragua. He soon became caught in shifting alliances and political treachery, not only in Central America but in the United States as well. He was shot by a Honduran firing squad in 1860.

In the 1860s the Keith brothers went into Central America and began building railroads. Minor Cooper Keith, the only brother who survived the climate there, not only built a railroad network but began selling bananas as well. In 1899 he founded the United Fruit Company which, for the next seventy years, was one of the most powerful companies in the region. It settled lands, created jobs, ran a large shipping fleet, and controlled railroads, ports, and other businesses. Keith and his successors did vitalize the area, but they have also been rightly accused of paying low wages to natives, interfering in local governments for their own advantage, and acting in hostile ways to outsiders in order to protect their monopoly of the banana industry. Few of their profits went into the countries that supplied the land and labor for their successes.

The Roosevelt Corollary

While United States citizens were active in Latin America, the government used the Monroe Doctrine to affirm its vested interests. A blatant claim to United States control was made by President Grover Cleveland in 1895. Britain then had a border dispute with Venezuela, and the Cleveland administration pointed out that it was difficult for any European power to rule a country 3,000 miles away. This was a disguised threat which, at the same time, affirmed United States control in Latin America.

In 1898, the United States entered the Cuban fight for independence from Spain. After the war, Cuba was made an American protectorate. In 1901, the United States Congress passed the Platt Amendment which forced Cuba to recognize this status, even writing it into a new constitution. The amendment allowed the United States to intervene in Cuba to preserve order or "Cuban independence," and it did step in—in 1906, 1912, 1917, and 1920.

A more formal interpretation of the Monroe Doctrine was announced in 1904 by Theodore Roosevelt, then President of the United States. Called the Roosevelt Corollary, it justified United States government intervention in any Latin American country in order to keep peace and ensure proper international relations. Revolutions and change of regimes in these countries, along with corruption, often affected the debts owed to foreign countries and nationals. Great Britain, Germany, and Italy attacked Venezuela in 1902 in an effort to force the collection of loans. The same thing happened in Santo Domingo (present-day Dominican Republic) in 1904. The United States was instrumental in settling both disputes. In Santo Domingo, the American government became a money collector for Europe and took control of revenues in that country in order to pay off creditors. Haiti followed in 1905 with the same arrangement. Then, as internal disturbances threatened the arrangements, the two countries on the island were occupied by United States troops, Haiti in 1915 and Santo Domingo in 1916. The troops were not withdrawn until 1934, but the countries remained under American customs supervision until 1941. Roosevelt was seeking to extend the Monroe Doctrine with his corollary, but to the governments and people of Latin American his "big stick" technique was only one more example of United States imperialism.

At the beginning of the twentieth century, the United States renewed its interest in digging a canal through Central America to connect the two oceans. The French had tried to do so in Panama but had failed. The United States government under Roosevelt bought out the French and then negotiated with Colombia to rent land rights through the area. Colombia did not like the financial terms and refused to negotiate. The Roosevelt administration then aided a Panamanian revolution against Colombia, bribed a few Colombian officers to stay out of the way, and sent a gunboat to Panama to make sure everything went according to plan. In return, the new Panamanian government gave the United States complete control of the proposed canal and a ten-mile-wide strip through Panama forever. The canal was finished in 1914, but by 1978 "forever" had run out. Panamanians came to resent the "Zonians," those Americans who lived the good life in that ten-mile strip. They became scapegoats for all of Panama's ills, and the accumulated resentment of the United States in Latin America focused on this spot. A new treaty was negotiated during President Jimmy Carter's administration. The canal is now a joint United States–Panamanian venture and in the year 2000, Panama will take it over completely, with assurances that it will be kept open to all nations.

Good Neighbors

Another Roosevelt, Franklin Delano, became president in 1933. He instituted the Good Neighbor Policy, whereby the United States government promised to keep its armed forces out of Latin America and to promote an increase of trade with the area. In the same year, the United States pulled the marines out of Nicaragua. They had been there first in 1909, then in 1912, both times to put down revolution and settle the problem of Nicaraguan finances. Then in 1925 they were back again. This time they stayed until 1933, spending a good deal of time trying to find Augusto Sandino and break up his rebellion. The marines helped establish the Nicaraguan National Guard during this period, and Somoza made his successful bid for power as its head. Thus, whether justfied or not, the United States is inevitably connected with the rise of the Somoza regime and the defeat of Sandino.

It was exactly this type of reaction that Roosevelt wanted to put aside, but his policy did little to change things. In fact, it was under his administration that the United States established military missions in Latin America, attached to the American embassies there. From this point on, the United States no longer simply intervened in Latin American countries but began to train the soldiers and police of the region. Part of this new posture grew out of the oncoming threat of World War II, when Roosevelt sought assurances that Latin American nations would remain neutral or join the Allied side.

An Old Doctrine, A New Problem

By the end of World War II, the United States had a new concern: communism in Latin America. With the onset of bad relations between the United States and the Soviet Union after 1945—the period generally known as the Cold War—the United States was determined to prevent the expansion of Soviet power in the world. Latin America, by historical and ideological tradition, was off limits to communism.

American governments made use of two basic methods in order to conduct the new policy. First, the CIA (Central Intelligence Agency) was used to carry on covert activities, such as training unofficial Latin American forces to overthrow or "destabilize" hostile governments. The CIA backed a Guatemalan force in the overthrow of the elected Arbenz government in 1954. The CIA also provided the money and training facilities for the Cuban exiles who took part in the unsuccessful Bay of Pigs invasion in Cuba in 1961. It was the CIA that supported anti-Allende factions with funds to carry on their strikes and demonstrations in Chile from 1970 to 1973. And the CIA has been responsible for supplying the anti-Sandinista guerrillas operating out of Honduras since 1981.

The second method was to support military regimes in Latin America and provide them with military aid. Such governments were viewed as more desirable than communist systems. In 1953, a year before the overthrow of Arbenz in Guatemala, Secretary of State John Foster Dulles advised President Eisenhower to award the Legion of Merit to General Pérez Jiménez, the ruthless dictator of Venezuela. Jiménez was held up as a model for all Latin American countries. In 1965, an American scholar determined that military aid given to Somozan Nicaragua at the time averaged $930 worth of equipment and training per soldier, while the annual per capita income was $205; in Guatemala, the ratio was $538 to $185. These figures reflected a doubling of United States military aid to Latin America after 1959, when Castro took power in Cuba. The estimated yearly average in the 1950s was $35 million; from 1960 to 1965, the average was over $70 million.

Also after 1960, programs were introduced that favored counterinsurgency training, including not only military studies but various civilian activities in the political, economic, and cultural spheres. Such training involved the armies of Latin America in nonmilitary activities, where they could be on the lookout for subversive elements. Latin American officers were trained at Fort Bragg, North Carolina, in psychological warfare, riot control, intelligence, and counterintelligence. In Central America, such troops formed part of the Central American Defense Council (CONDECA) which was established in 1964. CONDECA was an attempt to create joint military actions for collective security, especially where communist or subversive aggression was concerned. The council was linked to the United States through aid programs and American military missions attached to embassies in the countries.

The School of the Americas, run by the United States Army in the Panama Canal Zone, was a famous military training center. From 1936 to 1983, over 42,000 Latin American soldiers went through its programs, including Leopoldo Galtieri, who was president of Argentina during the Falklands invasion, and the recent head of the armed forces in Honduras, General Gustavo Álvarez Martínez. Every Latin American country had soldiers training there at one time or another. In September 1984, under the terms of the new United States–Panama treaty, the school closed its doors. If the United States wishes to continue to train soldiers, it will have to do so on North American territory.

Economic Aid

Along with military funding and training, the United States government had offered limited economic aid under Franklin D. Roosevelt, partly as a response to Latin American countries that joined the Allies. After World War II, such aid increased. President Truman initiated the Marshall Plan to revitalize Western Europe and also introduced an economic and technical program to help developing countries. Called Point Four, because it was the fourth point in Truman's 1949 inaugural address, where he first outlined the plan, it was a more intensive involvement by the American government in Latin America than ever before. It was dropped under Dwight D. Eisenhower, who became President in 1953. In the years he was in office, the United States government followed a policy of free-market economics. Private industry and banks were expected to provide the funds necessary to build up the economies of Latin America through investment and loans.

This policy aroused the ire of influential Latin Americans. They kept calling for international price agreements on their agricultural export products so they would no longer be subject to the ups and downs of the market, for more investment in technology, and for a development bank that would offer low interest loans and technical help for projects in their countries. The Eisenhower administration ignored these requests, believing they were functions of the private sector. When Vice-President Richard M. Nixon went on a state trip to eight Latin American countries in 1958, Washington was taken aback by the violent demonstrations he encountered along the way. Nixon was known for his anti-communist stance, and it was during the Eisenhower administration that the Arbenz government in Guatemala was overthrown with CIA help. Student leftists were believed to have led the demonstrations against Nixon, but such virulent anti-American feeling was displayed that a revision of policy began then. The first indication of this change was the establishment of the Inter-American Development Bank in 1959, one of the items Latin Americans had been calling for.

When John F. Kennedy became President in 1961, the Cuban revolution had already taken place. His administration sought to create an economic and technical aid program on a scale vastly greater than any such program that had come before. Called the Alliance for Progress, it also included social reform in its program and promised government funding up to $20 billion over a period of ten years. At the same time, the Kennedy presidency placed more emphasis on counterinsurgency training, the idea being to promote economic and social development under liberal-thinking leaders in Latin America and at the same time make it possible for them to defeat any communist guerrilla forces that might threaten their countries by armed attack.

Aid did increase during the Kennedy administration, and improvements were made, but there was less reform than hoped for. The military and the rich continued to play a major role in the countries and effectively blocked any important changes such as land reform.

After Kennedy's death in 1963, Lyndon Johnson became President. By 1965, Johnson had sent 20,000 troops to the Dominican Republic to avoid a take-over by a Castro-like regime. This act marked the beginning of a period of decline in United States economic interest in Latin America. From Johnson to Nixon and Ford, a period of fourteen years, Latin America received mostly statements of friendship rather than any new significant economic programs. Nixon did increase military aid on the advice of Nelson Rockefeller, who made an official trip through the area and reported back to the President. Rockefeller saw the military as a force for reform and a bulwark against communism.

During President Jimmy Carter's administration, from 1977 to 1981, there was greater interest shown in Latin America, but more as part of the Third World than as an area that might have a unique relationship with the United States. Carter's interest was in human rights, and his method of protecting those rights was to create economic pressure on oppressive governments by withholding aid. The process was not always successful, but it did help to bring the excesses of Latin American *caudillos* and generals to the attention of the world.

While the economic policies of the United States government toward Latin America waxed and waned in the period after World War II, American private enterprise maintained a strong presence in the area.

The Business of Business

In the nineteenth century, the British dominated markets in Latin America. By the beginning of the twentieth century, the United States had begun to displace British interests, taking over completely after World War I. Since Latin American countries were always dependent on agricultural, mining, and animal products for export earnings, they were forced to sell their goods in highly competitive markets. They needed their trading partners more than the partners needed them. They suffered severely in the depression of the 1930s, and many then decided to create an industrial base so as to be less dependent on imports. It was then that Latin American countries set up laws to cut down on imports in order to protect and encourage national industries and help them develop.

By the 1930s, United States companies had long been active in Latin America, owning outright mines, oil enterprises, and agricultural production in many countries or providing manufactured goods as import products. American and other foreign companies got around import restrictions by setting up their own factories in the countries under native names and partial ownership. Thus, as Josué de Castro, a Brazilian physician and nutritionist wrote in 1969, "Buyers, unaware that they are dealing with an American trust, order their electrical equipment from the Industria Electrica Mexicana, the little sister, in disguise, of the Westinghouse Electric Corporation." Copper mines in Chile, petroleum and iron mining in Venezuela and wool and cotton processing in Peru, automobile manufacture in Brazil and bananas in Central America are only a few of the areas where United States businesses have had strong investments, either openly or through shared ownership. Kennecott Copper, Standard Oil, Gulf Oil, United States Steel and General Motors, Sears Roebuck, Westinghouse, and United Fruit are some of the firms that are or have been in business in Latin America. By 1979, Latin America was the third largest market for the United States, after Western Europe and Canada.

On the other side, Latin America became more and more dependent on the United States as an export market. In 1912, the United States bought 12 percent of the goods exported from Latin America; in 1958 that figure had grown to 45 percent. And after World War II, United States investment in Latin America increased five times over a period of twenty-five years. Almost 80 percent of United States direct investment in Third World countries was restricted to Latin America and the Caribbean area by the end of the 1970s.

The objective of business is to make a profit, which is not considered wrong in a capitalist system. But some foreign companies underreported their profits, and this made Latin Americans suspicious of them. And these developing countries also grew anxious because foreign investments and foreign bank loans did not always accrue to Latin America's advantage. For instance, one report indicated that for the decade of the 1950s, Latin America received $47.4 billion in loans, gifts, and investments, but $20.9 billion went out of the region.

In *Global Reach*, Richard J. Barnet and Ronald E. Muller analyzed trade and investment data of multinational corporations in the Third World. They reported that in 1968, United States companies located in Latin America provided 40 percent of all manufacturing exports and took in over one-third of Latin America's imports from the United States. These companies systematically undervalued their exports from Latin America for local tax purposes and overvalued their imports to make higher profits. Such a procedure worked to the detriment of the Latin American countries concerned, both in terms of taxes collected and prices paid for items. In Colombia, one study determined that overpricing of imports stood at 155 percent in pharmaceutical firms, 16 to 60 percent in the electronics industry, and 40 percent in the rubber industry. The authors reported further:

> In Chile, according to Andean Common Market studies, overpricing ranges from 30 percent to more than 700 percent. According to the studies of Pedroleón Díaz, overpricing in Peru ranges from 50 percent to 300 percent and in Ecuador from 75 percent to 200 percent.

It was also not unusual for firms to report lower profits than they actually earned. Barnet and Muller cited a Peruvian Parliament commission, which determined that in the period from 1960 to 1965, the Southern Peru Copper Corporation, controlled by a United States company, reported net profts of $69 million to the Peruvian government, "whereas to the U.S. Securities and Exchange Commission the corporation had filed net profits of some 135 million dollars."

In answer to these reports the companies said that high risks called for high profits. They referred to military coups, which might bring nationalization of industries, and to kidnappings, which demanded high ransoms for return of executives. Barnet and Muller answered that in the decade from 1964 to 1974 only Cuba and Allende's Chile nationalized any United States companies in Latin America. On the other hand, military coups tended to benefit the companies:

In any event, one can afford a string of disasters if he is able to recover anywhere from 47 cents to $4 a year on every dollar he invests. To be sure, in a profit system it is unsporting to begrudge investors high profits. But the system has yet to evolve to the point at which everybody profits. One man's profit usually means another man's loss. The profits of the global corporations derived from poor countries, it must be said, are made at the expense of the people of those countries. The proposition that developed and undeveloped countries will get rich together through the expansion of global corporations is, at best, exactly half true.

Another writer, Joseph Ramos, an economist from Chile, is not so negative. He reported in 1981 that Latin America had grown at a rate of 5.2 percent a year for the previous thirty years, that per capita income had grown by 2.5 percent a year in the same period. This growth included agriculture and livestock, and there was also an increase in life expectancy and expansion of education.

In the 1970s, many Latin American countries began to exert tighter control on their economies once again. By 1980, as Ramos pointed out, "basic exports were nationalized or larger national control was exercised over them. This was the case, for example, in Chile, with its copper; in Peru, with its petroleum and sugar; in Panama with the canal; in Venezuela, with its petroleum." The most acute problems blocking further development in 1984 in Latin America were the huge foreign debt and inflation.

Such analysts as Ramos do not see economic and social problems arising from the presence of United States corporations in Latin America, or from their search for high profits. These analysts believe the problem stems from the fact that the Latin Americans themselves have never put their nations in order. Whatever gain these investors brought to the countries was never distributed throughout the population by those who held political power; it was not the responsibility of American corporations to do this. Instead, wealth remained in the hands of the very rich, who shared it with military officers and their middle-class followers.

Other Latin Americans, however, regard the United States as the agent that keeps the ruling elites in power. The United States government has too often appeared willing to sacrifice the good of Latin America to the profits of American corporations. As a result, Carlos Fuentes believes that Marxism is becoming an acceptable means of bringing peace and justice to Latin America. He also thinks the rise of Marxism indicates the people's rejection of the economic, political, and social system of the United States and of the local ruling elites who have espoused it:

. . . many Latin Americans feel that, whatever their shortcomings, the regimes in Cuba and Nicaragua have done what no previous governments in those

countries were capable of doing: mobilizing the people; finding solutions to problems of literacy, health, nutrition, and life expectancy; and at the same time imposing, at a high price, a politics of equality. . . . These are seen as enormous achievements in the light of a history dominated by privilege, extreme inequality, and callousness toward the needs of the majority. The association of the word "democracy" with governments incapable of coming to grips with these problems or indeed bent on maintaining the status quo only furthers the derogatory comparisons.

After Ronald Reagan became President of the United States in 1981, his administration set about resisting and defeating Soviet expansionism where possible. His Republican followers believed the Marxist "politics of equality" came at too high a price—namely Soviet control of Latin America. The Democrats, who held a majority in the House of Representatives, did not agree with the President's approach, believing instead that the problems were local and that the United States should allow for local solutions. At times the arguments reflected partisan politics and jockeying for power, and both Republicans and Democrats disagreed among themselves. Thus the two approaches reflected the history of United States involvement in Latin America. Central America again became a subject of concern and debate.

The Arguments Continue

President Reagan's first secretary of state, Alexander Haig, Jr., saw Central America as the focus of a growing confrontation between capitalism and communism, a struggle between the free world and totalitarianism. He saw Central America as the place where the resolve of the United States to resist communism and Soviet encroachment was to be tested; Haig and the President intended to pass that test.

In addition, the Reagan administration stated that Central America was of strategic importance to the United States. Some 50 percent of American shipping passed through the Caribbean, and the United States could therefore tolerate no hostile governments anywhere in the region. In wartime, an enemy could block sea-lanes and attack ships. Thus, the Soviet threat was very real.

Three countries played a major role in the strategy of the Reagan administration: El Salvador, Nicaragua, and Honduras.

The United States supplied El Salvador with arms and training to help its army defeat the communist guerrillas who were roaming the country and threatening its security. At the same time, open elections were held there to create a democratic government that would reduce military abuses and introduce needed social and economic reforms.

The United States also pressed the Sandinista government in Nicaragua to give up its Marxist regime and introduce a broader democratic system. There were to be no more Cubas in Latin America. The Sandinistas could share in a government, but free elections must determine who will govern, and civil rights must be enforced for all citizens.

Honduras served as a jumping-off point for United States covert action against the Sandinista regime. The nation served as a sanctuary from which the anti-Sandinista Contras could make incursions into Nicaragua. Honduras also became a reinforced military bastion from which to confront the communist threat in the other two countries. United States and Honduran military forces carried on massive joint maneuvers in the country, and new bases were built.

The United States described this increased military activity in Honduras and El Salvador as a "shield" for the growth of democracy there. These countries could not develop stable economies, duly elected governments, and improved social conditions unless they kept the communist revolutionaries at bay with strong armies. American military aid was backed up with economic aid.

George P. Shultz became secretary of state in June 1982, and he continued these policies under President Reagan.

Congressional Resistance

Many Democrats in the House of Representatives did not like the military approach of the Reagan government. They felt that the best way to ensure a lasting peace in Latin America was to get the guerrillas and the government in El Salvador to negotiate a settlement and then hold elections. Without the participation of both sides, they said, elections would be meaningless. They also said that the Sandinistas might be less militant and more open to change if the United States stopped supporting the Contras. Then the Sandinistas would have no armed threat on their northern border, and the United States would not be cast in the role of a major adversary.

President Reagan declared that his aim was not to overthrow the Sandinista government but to force it to change its policies. In December 1982, however, Congress passed a law forbidding any attempt by the United States to topple the Nicaraguan government.

Congressional Democrats also disliked the growing militarization of Honduras and the increasing presence of the American military forces there. They believed it could only lead to United States involvement in a war. They expressed fears about a new Vietnam War, in which American forces would be hopelessly bogged down.

Journalists, academicians, former government officials, retired military officers, and private citizens took one side or the other in articles, books, reports, letters to editors, and public debates. Some claim that the threat to United States sea-lanes in the Caribbean is more apparent than real. The United States would face such a threat in normal wartime whether communist governments existed in the area or not. Soviet submarines, for instance, operate worldwide and even now run along the United States coasts. The Soviets also know that the United States is the superpower in the Caribbean and will always act to protect its interests there. In the same way, the Soviet Union is the superpower in Eastern Europe. When Hungary, Poland, and Czechoslovakia rebelled at different times

and were suppressed, the United States condemned the Soviet Union in the press but did not
act.

Nevertheless, the President became upset because neither the Congress nor the country seemed
to be aware of what he believed was the global
danger confronting the Western Hemisphere in
Latin America. On April 27, 1983, he delivered a
major speech to a joint session of Congress on the
topic, which was carried to the nation on radio and
television. Both his speech and the Democratic re-
joinder showed that neither side had changed its
views.

The President called for $600 million in aid to
Central America, saying America had to meet the
"challenge to freedom and security in our hemisphere." He also said that if we in the United States
did not defend "ourselves there, we cannot expect
to prevail elsewhere. Our credibility would col-
lapse, our alliances would crumble, and the safety
of our homeland would be put in jeopardy." He
again accused the Sandinistas of exporting revolution in the area and called on them to give up
their control of Nicaragua. President Reagan also
reassured Congress and the nation that he had no
intention of sending American troops into combat
in Central America.

Senator Christopher J. Dodd of Connecticut delivered the Democratic response immediately after
the President's speech. He first declared Democratic Congressional opposition to any Marxist state
or Soviet military base in Central America, saying
"we are fully prepared to defend our security and

the security of the Americas, if necessary, by military means." But he called the military buildup in the area a "formula for failure" because it did not focus on real problems. He said that if Central America were not "racked" with poverty, hunger, and injustice, there would be no revolution. "But unless those oppressive conditions change, the region will continue to seethe with revolution—with or without the Soviets." He then asked that the "power and influence of the United States" be brought to bear on ending hostilities in El Salvador and Nicaragua and then "to work for a negotiated political settlement in Central America. He did not present the Sandinista government as a "model democracy or as a force for stability," but said that by backing the Contras the United States only strengthened the Sandinistas. Finally, he said,

> **we must restore America's role as a source of hope and a force for progress in Central America. We must help governments only if they will help their own people. We must hear the cry for bread, schools, work and opportunity that comes from *campesinos* everywhere in this hemisphere. We must make violent revolution preventable by making peaceful revolution possible. . . . Most important, this approach would permit the United States to move with the tide of history rather than stand against it.**

A New Commission

In an effort to reach some agreement on policy, some members of Congress called for a bipartisan commission to study the Central American issues and recommend a policy on which both sides would agree. The idea was taken up by President Reagan and on July 19, 1983, he appointed twelve members to a National Bipartisan Commission on Central America. The members were experts in such areas as banking, labor, political science, economics, law, and diplomacy, and there were equal numbers of Democrats and Republicans. The chairman was Henry Kissinger—an appointment that stirred up considerable attention and debate. Kissinger, who had been secretary of state under Richard Nixon, sees commuinism in terms of military containment and East-West confrontation. He has been closely connected with the overthrow of Allende in Chile in 1973. Kissinger has also been accused of promoting secret military operations during the Vietnam War. Both of these alleged actions demonstrate his belief in political and military strategy above all. There were some strong individuals on the panel—such as Lane Kirkland, president of the AFL-CIO, and Robert A. Strauss, an active Democrat and a participant in the Carter administration—but many observers believed that Kissinger would dominate the group.

The task of the panel was not specifically defined, but the members were expected to recommend a long-range policy that would take into account economic, political, and social change. The members interviewed experts and activists in the United States and traveled to Central America where they spoke to government leaders and citizens of six countries, including Nicaragua. They did not meet with any Salvadoran guerrilla leaders or with the Contras.

On January 11, 1984, Kissinger handed a 132-page report to President Reagan. It went over all the ground concerning present social and economic conditions in Central America, gave a thorough description of the endemic problems there, and suggested ways to overcome them. But it did not generate a bipartisan policy for Central America. Some claimed the report simply buttressed the policies of the Reagan adminsitration. But there were enough dissents appended to the report by members of the commission so that each side could use it to its own advantage. The split in policy on Central America did not end.

Although the commission noted Soviet intentions in the region and advocated continued military aid, it also called for a massive "five-year appropriation of $8 billion to pull the area out of its depressed state." It also acknowledged the efforts of four Latin American countries that have sought to end tensions in Central America.

The Contadora Connection

In January 1983, representatives of Mexico, Panama, Colombia, and Venezuela met on the Panamanian island of Contadora to discuss ways of achieving a peaceful solution to problems in Central America. Since then they have been known as the Contadora group, and in mid-1984 they were still actively pursuing their objectives: to seek dialogue at the "Latin America level" and to reduce foreign intervention in the area. Above all, they want to keep the East-West confrontation out of

Latin America. In early October 1983, the Contadora group presented a 21-point declaration of objectives that was accepted by Nicaragua, Honduras, El Salvador, Costa Rica, and Guatemala. Included in the points were limits on armaments, arms traffic, outside advisers (a reference to the American and Cuban presence in the region), and moves toward internal democracy and plural institutions.

There are actually three informal factions in the Contadora group: (1) the four original Contadora participants; (2) Guatemala, Honduras, and El Salvador, all of which see Nicaragua as a threat to peace and democracy, although there has been little of each in their own countries; (3) Nicaragua, which sees the other three as bases from which the Nicaraguan Sandinistas can be attacked. Costa Rica has generally maintained neutrality in the fighting, but usually sides with Guatemala, Honduras, and El Salvador where peace proposals are concerned. All three factions have their own proposals for settling the region's problems, but the basic 21-point agreement was signed by all.

The Contadora group has been an effective mitigating force on the local level, but has not achieved any specific results.

Standoff

Policy differences in Washington continue. Two events in Central America did give each side hope for a turn in its favor.

In March 1984, Honduran generals ousted General Gustavo Álvarez Martínez as chief of the armed forces. He had been an enthusiastic supporter of the United States military buildup in Honduras and became more and more involved in foreign affairs of the country. His removal was seen as an attempt by Honduran leaders to secure greater control of United States activity in the country and to step back from the growing military tension in the region.

The successful free election of José Napoleón Duarte in May 1984 gave support to the Reagan administration's continued economic and military aid to El Salvador. Because of human rights abuses, death squad activities, and military ineptitude and corruption, the House of Representatives had become less and less inclined to support such aid. Leaders in the House now believed that Duarte should have the aid he needed to help him bring his country out of its decline and continue to resist guerrilla attacks.

Resistance in Congress continued to block more aid for the Contras in their struggle against the government of Nicaragua. The rejection is viewed as a failure for the Reagan administration's policy to keep pressure on the Sandinistas to create a more democratic government. Opponents see it as a reduction of the military commitment of the United States in Central America and what they believe was a certain effort to overthrow the Sandinista regime.

On June 1, 1984, Secretary of State George P. Shultz attended the inauguration of President Duarte in San Salvador. Afterward, Shultz flew to

Managua, Nicaragua, where he held secret talks with Daniel Ortega Saavedra, coordinator of the junta there. Neither side conceded anything and publicly both Washington and Managua continued to accuse each other of aggressive tactics and bad faith. However, there were hopes that the talks would lead to some accommodations and a lessening of tension between the two countries.

Are these events simply momentary shifts in the fortunes of Central America, or do they represent a growing effort on all sides to reach some compromise and avoid further bloodshed or, even worse, a devastating war? Only time will tell. A number of democratic governments now exist in Central and South America. United States citizens and their government continue to disagree about policy toward Latin America, but they all want to see these democratic experiments succeed. They still cannot agree on how to ensure this, however.

What 6 Will Tomorrow Bring?

Latin America stands at the threshold of important changes. There are several paths it can take, depending on how forces in the region come to influence events. A number of these forces are indigenous, formed over the centuries. We have discussed some important ones: deep-rooted poverty; authoritarian traditions that have imposed themselves on societies; a centuries-old enervated religious structure that is seeking to renew itself; endemic, almost inbred political corruption; and a fiery revolutionary spirit that can cut across class and racial lines and explode with devastating results.

Other forces come from outside the region and seek to serve their own purposes there by whatever means possible. We have also described some of these: one is the Western countries that have taken huge profits from Latin America over the last 150 years without leaving behind much in the way of improvement; another is the ever-growing military presence of the United States, which regards Latin America as its "backyard"; still another is the socialist-Marxist ideology that has found acceptance among Latin American rebels seeking a model for their own revolutions.

The clashes that result when these forces meet, combine, or confront one another are making headlines in our newspapers today. They are being debated in the executive and legislative branches of our federal government. They are of deep concern to the nations in Europe, to the Soviet Union, and to the Third World for various reasons. Central America, in particular, seems to be shedding its blood without solving its problems. No one is sure what the future holds for the area or how that future will affect the rest of the world. One miscalculation on the part of the United States, Cuba, or one of the nations in Central America could lead the region into a war.

All these forces have to be watched for any indication of what the future might hold for Latin America.

First and foremost are the strongmen and generals, and, waiting in the wings, any political or social groups that may find it convenient to back them in possible coups. In the attempts now being made to create more open, democratic societies, some interests will suffer. The loss of privileges by the wealthy, the middle class, industrial or business groups, for instance, can drive them into the arms of the old power brokers; such disenchanted groups are the stuff of which military coups are made. And the military, for the most part, would gladly use these groups in order to regain power.

On a broader scale, the people's lack of a firm political commitment could also influence the course of events. White- and blue-collar workers, university students, intellectuals, and farmers—indeed, all the people in any country—will shift their loyalty as their stomachs and pocketbooks grow full—or empty. They may be Peronists one day and anti-Peronists the next; they may oppose Allende when he disrupts the economy, but later on, they may oppose the general they invited in to eliminate Allende. Those who seek their fortunes in these countries are usually sensitive to these moods and respond to them when the time is ripe. Such possibilities may be building in Argentina and Bolivia at the moment.

On the other hand, where the military rules we must look for the possibility that the same fickle population will force the generals to withdraw. In Chile, especially, an increase in street demonstrations could bring either harsh reaction by police and soldiers, or a withdrawal of the Pinochet regime. He cannot shoot the entire population, and the jails only hold so many people. The generals in Bolivia found this out in 1982. One might say that Paraguay is an exception, since the country is so tightly controlled by General Alfredo Stroessner. But after the general goes, who can predict what will happen?

In each country, repression has been achieved through the strongman and the military. This dilemma has been solved in only one country, Costa

Rica, a democracy in which the army was disbanded in 1948. Can it be solved in the same way elsewhere? Probably the best one can hope for is that the armed forces will be taught to stay out of politics and become a professional corps that sees itself as guardian of the country, not arbiter of its governments. There are younger officers in some countries who believe this is the army's proper function.

At the present time there are many countries under democratic rule in Latin America; others are moving in that direction. The question remains whether these countries can weather crises facing them long enough to establish strong traditions of democratic government. And how long is "long enough"? Ten years? Fifty years? A century? And what must be done in such a period in order to create a democratic tradition? It is not just a question of education and literacy, for Argentina and Chile achieved high levels of both years ago, and they also have predominantly urban, sophisticated populations.

Certainly the poverty common to all these countries must be eradicated, and the concentration of wealth in a few hands must be broken up. In addition, one of the needs among these populations—apart from personal safety, security, and good health—is participation in governing their countries. This is so in a large country like Brazil, where 55 million voters recently agitated for direct elections of the president. It is also true in little Uruguay, where the people defied their military leaders by staging strikes and demonstrations to dramatize their desire for political amnesty, freedom of the press, and better public services.

It may seem unrealistic to say the unruly crowds in Argentina and Bolivia want to participate in their governments. But, having been subjected for so long to government by revolution and coup, they simply do not yet recognize that there must be limitations to the means of effecting change. The street is no place from which to run a government, especially if a majority of your fellow citizens voted to put that government in office. This has been a hard lesson for Latin Americans to learn and probably will require more trial and error in the future.

Another force to watch is the formation of new types of social and political alignments. Will the leftists create a greater leveling of societies when they are elected or brought in by revolution? Will Marxists and communists predominate? Will they permit some selected democratic development, such as universal literacy, but lock society into a new authoritarian mold, permitting no one to criticize their policies or their rule? In truth, if such a development takes place, they would be acting no differently than past *caudillos* or generals. However, the fear they would invoke would not be of just another Latin American dictatorship, but of the Soviet Union and its expansionist policies. Cuba, with communist control of its citizens' lives, is the example opponents can immediately cite, regardless of the social progress made there.

It is on this point that debate is most acrimonious and events deserve careful attention. If the left takes over, one's country will no longer be free but in bondage to a superpower on the other side of the world, it is said. Better to have a general we know rule us at home than some "emperors" we have never seen. Here, then, is a paradox: while the Marxists are always linked to a discredited economic and political system in the USSR, they and the revitalized Catholic church are among the groups in Latin America that are truly intent on leading their countries out of poverty and out of their historical bind. It is the left in its totality—Marxists, socialists, liberals, reformed clerics, no matter what their social class—who are willing to share the heavy responsibility of finding a new way by which democracy can come to Latin America. No one can predict what that way will be: a traditional system in Argentina and a more radical approach in Nicaragua may both reach the same goal of justice and peace for all. It is quite possible that Marxists or socialists could attain the presidency in Brazil and Peru in the near future. No doubt the fate of Allende will be in the minds of all as these new leaders seek to make changes. The question is, will they be allowed to try?

The role of the United States in Central America has been significant over the last few years. The Reagan government has been committed to introducing democracy there, backed by a strong military presence—its own and the armies of its client states. Critics of this policy have claimed that it has only reinforced the rule of the generals. They say further that the policy has only succeeded in freezing the guerrillas out of the societies that spawned them and creating a half-free community behind a wall of bayonets. But armed fortresses do not make democratic societies; nor, the critics add, is it elections that count most in Central America at present. Elections can have meaning only after there is internal reconciliation of militant forces and easing of tensions on borders. Where countries are divided by arms, they have remained so before and after elections.

This can be true as well in Nicaragua, where claims of Sandinista-controlled elections have been raised by opponents. And President Reagan's policy received a fresh opportunity to test itself in the recent election of Salvadoran president José Napoleón Duarte.

Josué de Castro, a Brazilian physician, was co-editor of a book on radicalism in Latin America published in 1969. What he wrote then is stil valid:

> **Drained of its lifeblood and bursting with energy, Latin America, a continent in the throes of development, is a source of concern and a basis of hope. It has to accomplish a revolution and a synthesis. First, it must cast off a feudal yoke, destructive monopolies, acquire economic independence, and allay the hunger of stomachs and hearts. Then, it must reconcile the requirements of revolution with human respect and refrain from sullying the present in the name of a bright future.**

In 1992, Latin America will celebrate the 500th anniversary of the discovery of the new world by Christopher Columbus. Latin America has been a land of terrible, unrelenting suffering in those centuries; it has been a scene of anger, violence, pillaging, and an endless list of similar outrages. But it is today a land of energy, optimism, bravery, and belief in the future. In 1992, there will be much to celebrate.

It is time the Latin Americans were allowed to find their own paths in the world. It is time they were allowed to reconcile their internal forces in a manner all the people deem best for themselves. It is time they received back from those nations who have ignored or misused them in the past a sympathetic and honest helping hand toward the realization of their own goals. Let us hope that Josué de Castro's challenge will be realized and that a new era will see the fulfillment of the potential this great continent and its people hold.

Bibliography

The *New York Times, Washington Post, Los Angeles Times,* and *Miami Herald* are four newspapers that regularly report on current events in Latin America as seen by their reporters there. Only the *New York Times* has an index to its articles.

Some magazines, as well, provide reporting on Latin America, such as *The Nation, New Republic, Newsweek, Time,* and *U.S. News and World Report.* Lengthy articles can be found in magazines such as *Foreign Affairs, Current History* and *Commentary.* Two magazines that cover religious events are *Christianity and Crisis* and *Christianity Today.* A magazine that reports the view on the left is *NACLA Report on the Americas.* The best way to find magazine articles is through indexes like *Readers Guide to Periodical Literature* and *Magazine Index.*

There is no up-to-date book on the whole area of Latin America. For general background there is Lewis Hanke, *Modern Latin America: Continent in Ferment,* two volumes (Van Nostrand, 1959), and Ralph Lee Woodward, Jr., **Central America: A Nation Divided* (Oxford University Press, 1976). Thomas E. Skidmore and Peter H. Smith, **Modern Latin America* (Oxford University Press, 1984) covers the past along with the present but only for selected countries. Briefer views of the area are

*Books easiest to read

provided in William E. Carter, *South America* (Franklin Watts, 1983) and Patricia M. Markun, *Central America and Panama* (Franklin Watts, 1983). Byron Williams, *Continent in Turmoil* (Parents' Magazines Press, 1971) is also good.

Individual countries are covered by such works as the Land and People Series of Lippincott: for instance, Lionel Landry, *The Land and People of Colombia* (1970); J. David Bowen, *The Land and People of Chile* (1976); Alan Mark Fletcher, *The Land and People of the Guianas* (1966); other titles in the series deal with Argentina, Bolivia, Brazil, Central America, Cuba, Mexico, Peru, Uruguay, and Venezuela. While not up-to-date, these books describe problems that still exist.

There are several useful titles on Central America. Among them are Lila Perl, *Guatemala, Central America's Living Past* (Morrow, 1982); Glenn Alan Cheney, *El Salvador, Country in Crisis* (Franklin Watts, 1982). Marvin E. Gettleman and others have edited *El Salvador: Central America in the New Cold War* (Grove, 1981) which includes articles by citizens of the area as well as United States government personnel and American reporters and citizens. Two books that describe events leading up to the Nicaraguan revolution and the situation immediately afterward are Bernard Diederich, *Somoza and the Legacy of U.S. Involvement in Central America* (Dutton, 1981) and *Nicaragua: A People's Revolution* (EPICA Task Force, 1980). Susan Meiselas captures the revolution in photographs in *Nicaragua, June 1978-July 1979* (Pantheon, 1981). For Mexico see Lila Perl, *Mexico, Crucible of the*

Americas (Morrow, 1978). For Cuba, see Herbert L. Matthews, *Cuba* (Macmillan, 1964); Howard and Nancy Handelman, *Cuba Today: Impressions of the Revolution in its Twentieth Year* (American Universities Field Staff, 1978); *Impact of Cuban-Soviet Ties in the Western Hemisphere*, hearings held by the House Subcommittee on Inter-American Affairs (Government Printing Office, 1979). Keep in mind that the United States Congress issues reports of its hearings which can contain expert testimony on policy, summations of conditions in an area, and arguments among those present.

Coverage of the Catholic Church and its problems is in Penny Lernoux, *Cry of the People: The Struggle for Human Rights in Latin America* (Penguin, 1982). Henri J. Nouwen, *Gracias! A Latin American Journal* (Harper & Row, 1983) deals with grass-roots experiences by a Catholic priest.

For a close look at some recent strongmen see Tad Szulc, *Twilight of the Tyrants* (Holt, 1959); and Joseph A. Page, *Peron: A Biography* (Randon, 1983). Irving L. Horowitz, Josue de Castro and John Gerassi, editors, *Latin American Radicalism: A Documentary Report on Left and Nationalist Movements* (Random House, 1965) still contains good background material on radical attitudes and beliefs.

Index

About the Author

Robert Karlowich was born in Branford, Connecticut. He has a B.A. from New York University and a Doctorate in Library Science from Columbia University. Mr. Karlowich, who has been head of Slavic Acquisitions at the University of Illinois and at Columbia University, has long maintained an interest in communism in the contemporary world. The author, who lives in Pennsylvania, teaches at the Graduate School of Library and Information Science at the Pratt Institute.